SELECTED POEMS
1961-1994

Patrick Cullinan

Edited and introduced by Stephen Watson

Illustrations by Judith Mason

SNAILPRESS

S N A I L P R E S S
30 Firfield Road, Plumstead 7800

First published 1994
ISBN 1-874923-24-8

9/8/95

Cover design and illustrations by Judith Mason
Back cover photograph by Diane Cullinan
Typeset by User Friendly
Printed and bound by Interpak

CONTENTS

Introduction by Stephen Watson	ix
I 1961-1972	
Spring Burning	25
Thundershower	26
The Green	26
The Evangelists in Africa	27
Unseen Flame	28
Johannesburg 1902	28
Vultures	29
The Garden	30
Moths	31
The Walls of Naletale	32
The Quiet	33
North	34
Exiles	36
Devils	38
The Estuary. August 1964	40
The Beach, The Evening	42
Aspects of a Foreign City	42
The War	43
Nunc Dimittis	44
At Forty Odd	46
A Kind of Grass	47
II 1973-1979	
Filippo Argenti	51
M. le Vaillant	52
Madagascar	56
The First Hours	57
The Billiard Room	58
Spring coming: Zoo Lake	60
The First Danger	63
Grammar	64
On the Wild Coast	65
September at the Tuileries	66

The Mediterranean Idiot somnabulates 69
Prehistory, Catembe Ferry 71
Grand Hotel 72
Mkulu Kakhulu 74
We always greet you smiling 76
The Old Location 77
Not often 78
Johannesburg November 79

III Versions 1974-1994
The Age 85
Easter Transit 86
Two Mares 87
A God unknown 89
At the Cafe San Marco 94
Succulents 95
Being careful 95
Quartet 96
A Visitant 97
I don't know if God 98
In the Garden 99
Wind on the Half-Moon 100
The Letter unwritten 101
The House on the Frontier 102

IV 1980-1994
To have Love 107
A Dream of Guests 107
Again 109
Gramary 110
The Dust in the Wind 111
The First Far Beat 111
Homage to David Livingstone Phakamile Yali-Manisi 112
Sorry, Douglas 113
Sir Tom 114
That 116
The Bestiary 119
The Shell 119

The Text	120
The Astrologer	122
Honey	123
Laura	123
The Bowl of Tulips	123
The Abandoned Farm	124
The Map	125
Venice	126
Nativity	127
Mimesis	128
For Rebecca, born at Midwinter	130
Etruscan Girl	133
Notes	137

By the same author:

The Horizon Forty Miles Away (poetry)
Today is not Different (poetry)
The White Hail in the Orchard (poetry)
Lionel Abrahams: A Reader (editor)
Robert Jacob Gordon 1743-1795 (historical biography)
Selected Poems 1961-1991: A limited edition of forty books, Artists' Press, Johannesburg.

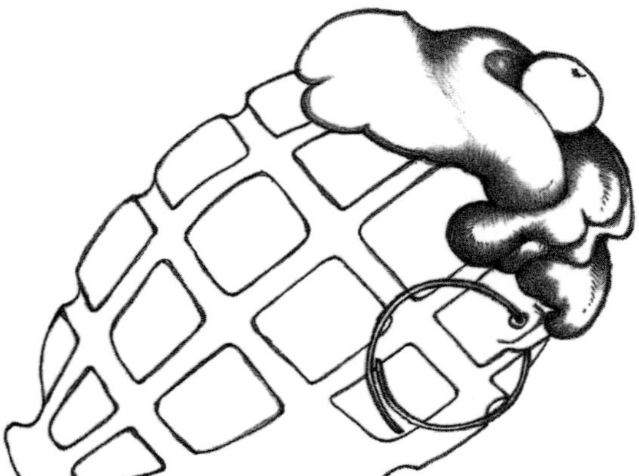

INTRODUCTION

When it is borne in mind that the usual relation of the South African poet to the realities of his or her native land has been rather like that of a fly to fly-paper – messily close and mostly fatal – then that single feature which at once distinguishes the poetry of Patrick Cullinan becomes more apparent. While he is undeniably a South African poet, often writing from the very midst of this complex fate, even the earliest of the poems selected for this book shows the extent to which he has always stood at a certain distance from what is commonly understood to be the heart of the South African matter.

Although there are poems of his which – for example – deal with those anxieties which are common currency in the psychic life of South Africans, he has never paid much heed to that indigenous Berlin Wall, supposedly dividing the political from the non-political, which critics have used in the last few decades to separate local poets into good and bad, patriots and traitors. Moreover, Cullinan's work, especially when taken as a whole, clearly follows a line of development, a trajectory, which carries the reader far beyond that local terrain, a good deal more sticky than fly-paper, widely regarded as the only authentic subject-matter for the South African poet. Above all, it is this which has ensured his poetry's uniqueness, its marked difference from that of his contemporaries. It is also this which, not surprisingly, lies behind the unusually distinctive place he has made for himself in South African poetry.

As with many another writer, his origins explain a great deal. Born in Pretoria in 1932, Patrick Cullinan was precipitated straight into the still colonial ethos of the upper middle-class of English-speaking South Africa. This accidental destiny, the privilege and painfulness of which would later be suggested in some of his best poems (principally, 'The Billiard Room' and 'Sir Tom'), also determined the type of schooling he was to receive. In the immediate aftermath of World War II, when scarcely out of boyhood, he was despatched overseas to the English public school, Charterhouse. Later, he was to complete his education at Magdalen College, Oxford, where he took a degree in Modern Languages, becoming fluent in both Italian and Russian languages and literatures. Thus to a South African boyhood – in part the generic, barefooted kind – was added some of the more complex elements of what T. S. Eliot once called 'the mind of Europe'.

In a virtual colony such as South Africa was then, an intellectual inheritance like his could be regarded as a dubious one, generating the kind of loyalties that remain eternally divided between Johannesburg and London. Not that this was much the case with Patrick Cullinan. But when in the early 1950s he turned down a job as Reuters correspondent in Moscow and decided to come back to South Africa for good, he was returning secure in the possession of something not easily achieved by more recent generations of South African poets. Already, by virtue of his European education, a kind of distance, a space, had opened up between himself and his native land, rendering him less vulnerable, as a writer, to the many local varieties of parochialism; and, perhaps most of all, to a political ethos that was soon to spread over the country like some vast, collective incubus, causing many a mind to contract beneath its weight.

In this he was truly fortunate. For a sensibility that had been steeped in Dante, as his was at Oxford, even the hell of South Africa post-1948 must have seemed one of the more elementary forms of Purgatory. For someone like himself, well-versed in the Russian poets of the Silver Age, and particularly in what became of the lives of Mandelstam, Tsvetayeva, Akhmatova, and Pasternak under the hand of Stalin, the enthusiasms of politics, including the ardours of commitment, were to appear in a more ambiguous light than many a more recent South African writer has been able to recognise. In short, Patrick Cullinan's imagination – that mysterious yet necessary faculty which Wallace Stevens once defined as the mind's pressing back against reality – was from the beginnings of his career more than a little removed from local passions, and thereby fortified in its work of resistance.

The necessity for this resistance will appear the more obvious when it is remembered what the specifically South African reality of the forties and fifties amounted to. In essentials it was not that distinct from the one which another colonial, prodigal son, Patrick White, was dismayed to re-encounter when he returned to Australia in the late 1940s after a long period of expatriation:

In all directions stretched the Great Australian Emptiness, in which the mind is the least of possessions, in which the rich man is the important man, in which the schoolmaster and journalist rule what intellectual roost there is, in which beautiful youths and girls stare at life through blind blue eyes, in which human teeth fall like autumn leaves, the buttocks of cars grow hourly glassier, food means steak and cake, muscles prevail, and the march of material ugliness does not raise a quiver from the average nerves.

In a context such as this, its ugliness only exacerbated by racial bigotry, anyone interested in books and writing, let alone the more dubious vocation of poetry, could not but have felt his or her distance. But I also suspect that the possible benefits, even the virtues, of preserving this distance would not have seemed negligible. In any case, what we find throughout the body of Patrick Cullinan's work is an imagination actively engaged in pressing back against the confines of the local cultural climate (with its gods of Money, Muscle and Machinery) and thereby asserting its difference, its distance, from it.

This manifests itself in more ways than can be enumerated. In the first place there is his language. From the outset Cullinan has resisted the many stylistic clichés of English South African poetry. In his work there are neither zebras nor zebra-crossings; none of the artificial fires of poetry, nor its artificial tears. Having early reacted against the influence of Dylan Thomas, he provides few rhetorical thickets in which one's consciousness might easily, and lazily, immerse itself. Cullinan's voice is new by virtue of a lyricism so restrained, pruned back, even straitened, as to sound deliberately anti-lyrical, close to a form of anti-poetry. Almost every poem of his lies on the page like some well-gutted creature, nothing but the spine left along with the essential knots of bone that hold it in place. Even when he writes what is ostensibly a landscape poem (like 'The Dust in the Wind') included here, his intense and sensual bond with that high, bare country in the Eastern Transvaal, at the northern end of the Drakensberg, does not culminate in any effort to reproduce the visual splendours of the land; or even in the attempt to produce the linguistic counterpart of a country mostly bones. In fact, so spare is the verbal texture of his poems that the reader might well come away from them with the impression that they are strangely context-less, somewhat like a stateless person. But this is only because it is characteristic of Cullinan to register the presence, including the pressures, of South Africa differently, indirectly. The land is there, in his poems, chiefly in a language which is a consistent kind of anti-mimesis, a verbal minus-sign set against a place whose rhetorical excesses, in literature as in life, have not ceased to flourish throughout his career.

The poetry, too, is insistently there. It inheres most obviously in the precision of Cullinan's cadences, his short lines rhythmically weighting each word with such sureness that to read one of his poems is to feel the individual words themselves inheriting a new gravity, the medium of time in which they move a slowed-down density. This can be seen in any number of examples, not least in these stanzas from his 'North':

> On watch tonight I stare
> At one point in the blank sky.
> A star glitters. At once
> It is there, as though my staring
> Brought it out.
> Was it ordained?
> This star is in the South.
>
> The women and the children sleep
> In the warm heart of the camp.
> It is not death I fear
> But the thought that birth will stop.
> I fear the end of my people.

In a poem like this history is re-cast as myth, ancient fears being given an archetypal resonance whose possible reference goes way beyond those tribes which feared extermination during the Mfecane in the nineteenth century. Here, too, another feature of his work is apparent. Patrick Cullinan is a poet who uses history – something of a rarity in a country where the past is simply not a going concern for the majority of its inhabitants. He is a writer in whom an historical sense is acutely alive, his awareness of the past entering his work in a thousand different ways. Whether he is quoting from Dante, referring to the tradition of European painting, or re-shaping an incident in African history to form an ironical parable, for him the past is anything but so much disposable baggage. In his longest poem to date, the eighteenth-century French explorer, François le Vaillant, speaks on a far from exhausted topic when he ruminates years later on the significance of his travels in South Africa:

> I said and say again:
> The Fabulous was quite destroyed
> And in its place I set the truth.
> I made the country real, a normal place.
> Romantic, I agree, and odd but
> Savage the right way at last. I showed
> There were no Giants, club-footed or one-eyed.
> Who now denies that Pigmies are small men?
> Monomatapa, Vigite Magna have disappeared
> From the maps; and where I travelled
> That continent it is not dark.
> I say the best minds of the age
> Have made my Africa their own: my Truth
> Feeds their Imagination. I have shown
> That men in skins move in a certain
> Landscape, are men like us, have names:
> Confused, they love and hate.

In other words, it is through history itself that that mythical continent called Africa, long a prey to every alien's darker and more outlandish fantasies, may be made into a real place once more.

His more obviously contemporary, even political, poems are also quite distinct. Although there are occasional pieces like 'Spring Coming: Zoo Lake' in which Cullinan can be provoked by the insecurities proverbial amongst his kind, he is rarely, if ever, the poet-historian of white English-speaking South Africa, its uneasy privileges and threatened life-style. Many a fellow-poet has been obsessed with questions of identity, particularly the lack of any assured sense of this in his or her own kind. But to Cullinan it has never been an imperative concern that most white English-speaking South Africans have no more roots than an air-plant. 'We were native from the start', his dispossessed colonials declare, ironically, in 'Exiles'. And it is in such a poem that we can feel the force of that distinctive weapon which Cullinan uses most frequently in pressing back against the high farce and inhumanity of the South African social order.

Whereas the majority of South African poets, English or Afrikaans, have responded to the country's apartheid years with an intense passion, a close commitment, Cullinan has tended to respond through that other form of passion which deflates rather than inflates: the mode of irony. Frail as its effects might be, it has not ceased to have its place in a country whose citizens are amongst the world's more compulsive secessionists from reality. Nor is it surprising that it should feature so prominently in his work. More often than not, irony goes hand in hand with a habit of mind that is not that common in South African poetry before Cullinan. He is a poet of wit, the word itself being one of the most favoured in the vocabulary that he has made his own. This means more than that he believes in Pope's 'Nature to advantage dress'd', or, as the dictionary might tell us, in 'the utterance of brilliant or sparkling things in an amusing way.' Wit assumes the cardinal value it has in his work because it is the hallmark of a sceptical intelligence, prepared to disbelieve its own experience as well as that of others, free to conjure other worlds, the constant antagonist of the *ideé fixe*. It is one of the means through which the mind detaches itself from the confines of any social reality. In a country noted for its failures of understanding – and of all things South Africans regularly fail to understand, irony is probably the chief one – the very movement of mind, the wit, found so often in a Cullinan poem serves as a kind of judgement, even a condemnation, of an entire nation's slovenly mental hygiene.

At the same time, one cannot mistake that undertone of anguish that starts building through some of his poems, particularly in the late seventies, and culminates in the tortured lines of 'Grammar' and other pieces like 'Johannesburg November'. This is something which is latent in Patrick Cullinan's work from the start. For all the wit, the ironies, dark shadows fall across even the earliest of his poems, threatening their sophistication, troubling their composure. These are only partly, however, those shadows cast by politics. It is much more common for Cullinan to be concerned with the nightmares inside the self rather than those which might be figured in any physical or social landscape. The horror of the vultures in his poem of that name lies not in the predatory nature of the birds themselves, but something more perturbing, perhaps elusive, which is imaged in the psyche:

> It is as though
> Some horror
> Of your own had, falling,
> Snapped its ugly neck.

It may even be something more than a personal matter, one sign of a shift in a culture's deeper concerns, that Africa appears in his work as anything but that fearful monolith both adored and hated by earlier poets. Coming long after the colonial period and its self-confident extroversion, it is that ambiguous inner country of the mind, its uncertain frontiers and ever-present darknesses, which obsesses these poems.

Equally often, there is on the horizon of Cullinan's world something ominous building. Usually it finds its referent in an approaching storm or the sound of thunder, but the precise threat is less defined than any aspect of the weather. His is a poetry haunted by an oppressive sense of some great unvoiced, and no doubt voiceless, disquiet. Poem after poem is alive with the presence of unquiet spirits. Sometimes, as may be expected, it is the rock of politics on which his poems founder. But most frequently, it is something less definable, more sinister, fearfully other, like that which is superbly adumbrated with all the sub-verbal apprehensions it gives rise to in the last stanza of his 'The Walls of Naletale':

> The sun goes, the sky is big with rain
> And there is thunder. Not loud
> But a persistent mutter from the north,
> Intermittent, like the beat of drums,
> Remote but coming nearer.
> And we who stand here silent
> Feel the steady pulse-beat of our blood
> As something alien. We stare
> At shattered walls and bush,
> Knowing something more than fear,
> Dread perhaps, the first slow creeping edge
> Of mystery:
> Cold-blooded awe.

Zimbabwe might be the immediate context here, but the more constant theatre for Cullinan's poetry is one which makes no reference to geography. This is especially evident in his love poetry. It is the universal existential predicament that is stressed in the early poem, 'Unseen Flame', in which to love

> ... is to know
> You cannot change enough,
> Or have the quality
> Of unseen flame;
>
> It is to know
> You cannot love enough.

Similarly, the personal holocaust of a love lost becomes the characteristically impersonal four lines that is 'To Have Love':

To have love and then lose it:
the white hail in the orchard
lying with leaves it has stripped
and the storm moving away.

A poem, clearly, which might have happened anywhere; which could have emanated from Japan in the seventeenth century as much as South Africa in the twentieth.

But this is not all that emerges from his love poetry. With the exception of a few later poems like 'The Map' or 'The Abandoned Farm', it is immediately evident that Cullinan is seldom a poet of fulfilled love or reciprocated passion. In this area of his work, it is more often a sense of being 'by love outcast', of 'mortal disquiet' (two phrases from the poem 'Not Often A Night'), which tends to predominate. Here, again, the note struck is one of unease, something almost on the verge of anguish. For Cullinan, the recognition of that which is mortal, transient, inherently faulty and failing, is woven into the fabric of his love poetry far more insistently than any strand of eroticism might be.

And not without reason. For not only does this emphasis relate him to a literary tradition wider, if not older, than any that has existed in South Africa, but it also serves to underline the single feature which, perhaps above all, distinguishes his poetry. If love poetry occupies an important place in his work as a whole, it is because love itself, as Joseph Brodsky once put it, 'is a metaphysical affair whose goal is either accomplishing or liberating one's soul: winnowing it from the chaff of existence.' More than anything else, I believe it is this which interests Patrick Cullinan. He is, first and foremost, a metaphysical poet.

In fact, it is the consistent presence of the metaphysical in his poetry, as well as its obvious importance for him, which explains why his work has followed a trajectory that has carried him far beyond South Africa and the often narrow concerns of many another South African poet. It is largely this which has made any attempt to label Cullinan as a member of this or that school of poetry in this country so very difficult, and invariably misleading. Crossing or bypassing any line of division between what is supposedly African or European, a metaphysical aspect has rapidly become the hallmark of his imagination at its most distinctive, establishing itself as the chief means through which his mind has pressed back against both local and other realities. This is all the more remarkable in the South African context. For it is hardly an exaggeration to say that of all the barren areas in English-language poetry in South Africa over the last few decades, it is precisely that which is designated by the word 'metaphysical' which has been the most scorched. South Africans are known for politics, not for matters of the spirit. Yet it is particularly in this area that Cullinan's work has flourished. It is a metaphysical or spiritual bias that is the distinguishing mark of almost all his best work from the past decade. It informs poems as various as 'That', 'Venice', 'Mimesis', 'For Rebecca, Born at Midwinter', and 'Etruscan Girl'. Moreover, one suspects it is his own metaphysical needs that lie behind the type of work he has chosen to translate in Section III of this book, especially the large number of pieces by that God-haunted Italian poet, Eugenio Montale. In this area, as in many others, it is as though Cullinan has been concerned both to acknowledge that a hunger for spirituality is an indispensable longing of the human psyche, and also to find a channel, if not a resting-place, for an impulse which, given contemporary circumstances, has been all but homeless.

To call anyone a metaphysical poet today is to make a claim at once large and vague. Certainly, Patrick Cullinan's poetry contains no obvious moments of ecstasy, God being apprehended in all existence around him. Nor is there much evidence of a traditionally religious sensibility and its lifelong search for contact with the fleeting presence of the divine. In relation to such matters, I suspect it is Cullinan's version of Montale's 'A Letter Unwritten' that speaks for him – as it does for most of us:

> I cannot go,
> I cannot turn my face again to you.
> The evenings spread;

night will not end –
it burns like a scarlet forge
and prayer is torture.
                                        Even now
the bottle cast upon the sea
has not reached you; it floats
in surges of water and rock. The waves
break and are empty, the surf uncurls
at the end of the earth.

Like the Italian whom he reveres, Cullinan is a poet acutely aware that whilst men and women may need a metaphysics, they might no longer be able to have one. Or not, at any rate, in the latter half of the twentieth century.

Still, the need is there, entering into the fabric of many of his poems. It is there most obviously in the insistence with which his imagination turns to those black holes, death and historical transience, exploring that which gives rise to metaphysical needs and very often defeats them as well. It is present in an individual poem like 'That', most especially in its exploration of the ancient belief that ultimately the act of naming and the religious impulses are one and the same. Less obviously, the impulse is implicit in the frequency with which Cullinan's imagination is engaged in reaching after something which he cannot locate socially, intellectually, or even aesthetically. It is why, ultimately, his poetry is just not that interested in the South African quotidian, the evocation of the beauties of local landscape, and so forth. More than anything else, it seems his imagination seeks a ground which is evidently not to be found on any physical soil or in any map.

As this aspect of his work has assumed more and more importance, so have his poems become more modernist in their aesthetics. Even in 'Mimesis' there is no concern to produce an accurate verbal representation of an external reality. The landscape that becomes of ever-more interest to him is one which is made chiefly by words. On the one hand, this might be expected. Poets tend to be among the more word-obsessed of mortals, their chief ethical concern often being the purification of their tribe's forever contaminated language. But in Cullinan's case, it is equally apparent that many of his poems circle back on their own substance, words, for the reason that their focus is entirely other than some reality 'out there' which he seeks to capture realistically. And this is inevitable. In proportion as your goal is metaphysical, so will your conception of language, and the purpose of words, change.

Metaphysical, too, is the anchor which his imagination finally insists upon. Any reader of this book will notice how, especially in recent years, more than a few of Cullinan's poems have become meta-poems – that is to say, poems about poetry and the act of 'making' itself. Evidently, this is not because he is much taken with the self-conscious task of questioning his own practice, even as he practises it, in that manner which is almost a cliché of modernity by now. Rather, he has grown increasingly fascinated by what it is that makes for art, what specifically makes for that mysterious act of transmutation which transforms words, giving to them that effect of linguistic grace which we call poetry. And he has done so all the while implying that the imagination at its peak powers is naturally, even necessarily, metaphysical, and that any hope of wholeness, in art or life, may not be possible without its operations.

This finds its most memorable definition in 'Etruscan Girl', the final poem in this selection. It is one whose verses press towards the borderline of faith, towards the edge of that eternal 'as if' (or 'as though') which is the form that the faith intrinsic to poetry most often takes:

> And the figure half turns
> to stare at me,
> as though I
> could give a name:
> as though death did not
> repeal identity,
> as though there were
> a body there,

a spirit that I must see,
clearly.

And I try to imagine
those who called
the craftsman in,
the maker,
saying to him:
You knew   , you knew her well,
make her for us, make her
as we knew her in this life.

And it was
as he had seen her last,
sitting outside the house,
debonair in the morning,
plaiting her hair in the sun,
the hands and fingers quickly
pushing in and out
so closely that
the moment and the movement
fused:
and the maker saw
that they were one.

'Etruscan Girl' not only exemplifies Patrick Cullinan's art, but is also exemplary in its fulfilment of what I take to be the point, the most basic purpose of poetry, whether ancient or modern, South African or otherwise. Jorge Luis Borges, in one of his lesser-known poems, 'Elvira de Alvear', speaks of 'the gift of verse' and defines this gift quite simply, unforgettably, as that

> Which works to change real suffering into
> Music and to sound and to symbol...

'Etruscan Girl', likewise, epitomises this process. Behind it, too, lies that mysterious form of energy, that 'gift of verse', which will be found in abundance in Patrick Cullinan's poems.

Stephen Watson, Cape Town, January 1992

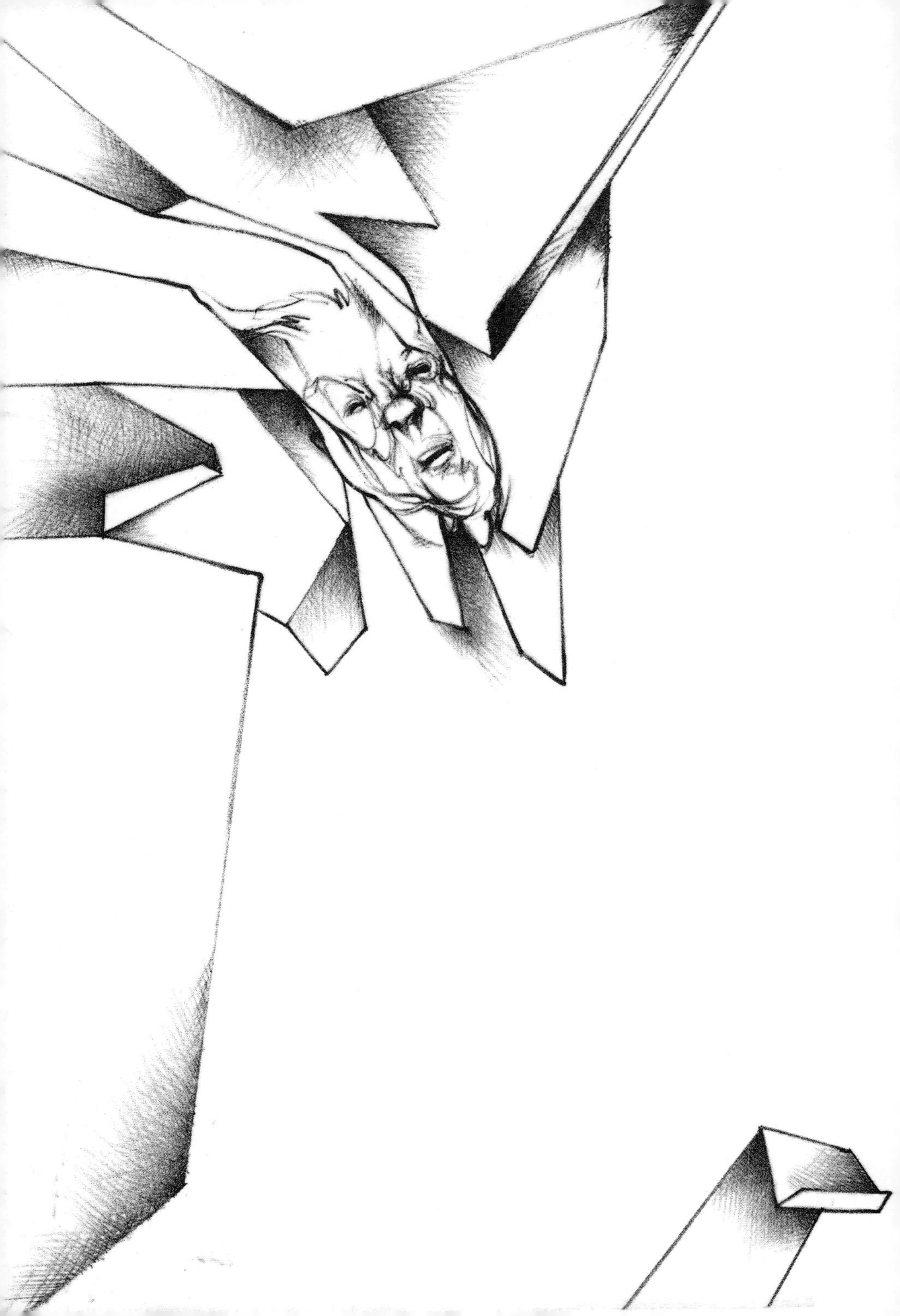

I

1961 – 1972

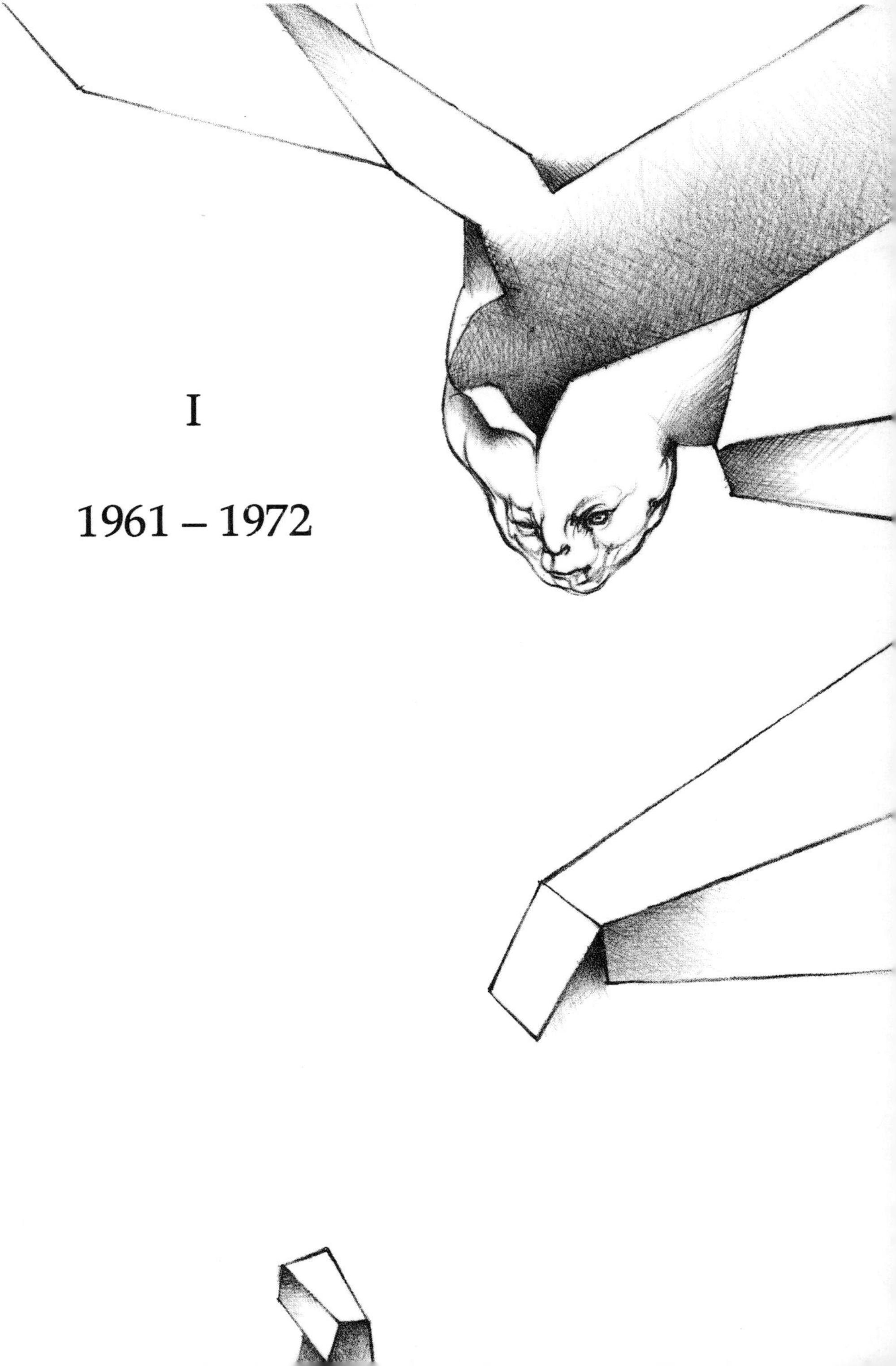

SPRING BURNING

Late in the afternoon:
Before the rain,
Before the summer,
A dead branch bursts –
Blazes at the tip.

A boy runs forward
From the men,
And dropping flame like seed
Sows the hills with fire.

And when the rain breaks
In the mountains,
He will see that flame
Go green through grass,
Grow fat in the bellies
Of his father's oxen,
Grazing slow and red.

And through his life, his dreams,
Fire will be his knowledge:
Will glow there bright in innocence,
And burn with fury through his age.

THUNDERSHOWER

When the rain, the first real rain of the year
Flashes on our black tin roof, we smile across
The room and know, surer than the calendar,
Twelve months have passed: and yet there is no loss.

We only remember how small we grow
At this sound: how a child is warm in bed
And hears the same rain heard a year ago.

The air is warm. The green days lie ahead.

THE GREEN

The beasts lie down
and they shine.

There is more grass
than they can eat.

Each day the sky
rumbles its swollen
guts,
and drops.

There is fat in the land,
meat.

THE EVANGELISTS IN AFRICA

Tapping a light drum,
The Evangelists
Are walking down the road
In white overalls,
Carrying branches:
Calling the world,
This Sunday morning
After the rain,
To walk slowly,
To whisper 'Hallelujah'.

Those who go with you
Seize a branch,
And somewhere deep in grass,
Along the river,
Make a church
To sing the truth:
The Hallelujah,
And know at once together
More of charity,
More of other men.

You move around the hill
And the thudding drum
Grows weaker:
This is the day of praise,
The sun is stronger,
And all the people
Living here sing
The creation, or make
Men out of branches
After rain on Sunday morning.

UNSEEN FLAME

Love is the changing day by day
Of life: it is a fire
Burning in sunlight,
Invisibly changing.

And love is to know
You cannot change enough,
Or have the quality
Of unseen flame:

It is to know
You cannot love enough.

JOHANNESBURG 1902

After the war, when we got back
To the house, my father came with
Cherry branches, a wagon full,
And I remember how glad we were:
Because till that day
We had never seen
Green branches with red cherries.
It is something I shall not forget.
I also remember how the soldiers
Took my matchboxes
That were hidden in a special drawer.

VULTURES

Below the krantz the heat stops
And in the shadow
Cracked bones and feathers pile.
Cold water oozes from the rock.

Dropped from its nest,
A hundred feet above,
A young bird hangs
Suspended from a bush.

Carrion already, the breast
Trembles under flies:
The beak gapes
In rictus.

It is as though
Some horror
Of your own had, falling,
Snapped its ugly neck.

Look close. Then go.
Walk into the heat.
Look into the light as though
All light had just begun:

Against blue air
The vultures circle.
Turning like flies
Across the sun.

THE GARDEN

Perfect? Almost. The roses blow
On long green lawns, the marble steps
Are guarded by glazed, heraldic dogs.
As a guest once said: 'The eye flows'.
And so it does, past pool and pool-room,
Border, vista, park
To hills which in the distance throb
With royal shades of purple.
But somehow the guests are uneasy.
The garden is not given, cannot be
Consumed like Scotch or good cigars,
Or Cherry Duckling Flambé
(A speciality of the house).
No, the garden can't be taken, so
Back they go indoors and, if polite,
Write long letters thanking him.
Some, the more sensitive, cannot sleep.
The night-long susurration
Of a water sprinkler
Can cause insomnia.

He came one day for the first time.
A new possession. Looking up
From a drink, dictating, he saw
That it was good, as it should be;
But for one thing:
It seemed to him
The birds screamed too much,
Were bright with 'vulgar' colour.
Luckily, then and there,
The Resident Director,
Sensing a dilemma, said: 'It's quite
All right, Sir, here,
In this country,

All birds cry like that:
Experts admit the hue is "gaudy".'
The boss nodded and noted the fact.
Like God resting
On the seventh day,
He knew it was not perfect
But decided to leave it like that.

MOTHS

They pack and fill
The covered lamp
Above the stoep
Like angels round
The Lord.
            Those
Who reach
The burning wick
Fall blinded.
Their white wings beat
Upon the ground.
            And there
A frog as fat
As Satan squats,
His body pulsing.
He gulps them
While they flutter
And makes no sound.

THE WALLS OF NALETALE

The old man shouts, claps his hands
And there is nothing:
A long hole
Deep in the rock,
A windpipe choked with pebbles.

And sweating in the sun,
We stood and listened:
Perhaps beneath the walls,
The arrow-patterned strips of stone,
We might have called and heard
A leopard cough, close, like a man:
We might have seen a snake
Suddenly,
Uncoiling,
Black,
Where no snake moved before.

But the old man fears his dead:
Knowing they whirr like insects
Round these trees and walls.
He claps his hands, shouts 'Mambo!'
He will not join them yet.

The sun goes, the sky is big with rain
And there is thunder. Not loud
But a persistent mutter from the north,
Intermittent, like the beat of drums,
Remote but coming nearer.
And we who stand here silent
Feel the steady pulse-beat of our blood
As something alien. We stare
At shattered walls and bush,
Knowing something more than fear,

Dread perhaps, the first slow creeping edge
Of mystery:
Cold-blooded awe.

THE QUIET

You said: *We must be quiet,*
We must listen.
But the long coloured lines of books
Get brighter,
The storm comes nearer,
Trees bend outside. Again the
Long beat of thunder:
And I can only hear
This uncalled drama.

But now the noise and colour stop.
A door bangs,
A child cries.
The afternoon is flat again
With ordinary sounds.

And I can begin to listen,
To be quiet.
To start hearing something
Nearer than I think.

You are right. You are right:
Between the long beats of thunder,
Before the rain really comes down.

NORTH

This morning we moved North again
Through strange bush.
We know the enemy still follows:
By night we see their fires,
By day their dust.

The old men talk, still,
Of our ancestors from North:
About the rich forests
And swarming game,
And of our return
Which is ordained
In the stars.
I see no sign of this North.
There are smaller trees
And unknown roots, more snakes
And fewer birds.
On a long journey
The land must change.

I think they will cut us off tomorrow.
There was dust this evening
On our right flank. Is it because
They do not want to fight
Among the hills ahead?
Mountains were our country:
They fear ambush and they are right.
There is no mercy between us:
They are so many.

On watch tonight I stare
At one point in the blank sky.
A star glitters. At once
It is there, as though my staring

Brought it out.
Was it ordained?
This star is in the South.

The women and the children sleep
In the warm heart of the camp.
It is not death I fear
But the thought that birth will stop.
I fear the end of my people.

EXILES

We shall try not to remember
The politics, the quarter truths
That made a total truth to us.
We shall try to remember our own
Temptation, when we had the power
And used it: when we had
It like a handkerchief
In the corner of our sleeves.
And if there was something absurd
About tennis on the equator,
It was the absurdity we drowned
With long drinks in the evening.

It is true: they have a personality.
But not, it seems, the one we saw.
Can any race have two
Personalities? There is something
Mad about facts when they diverge.
We remember what we saw. We knew them.
We knew them well enough to want their good.
And now we talk too much about it.
The dialects bore our countrymen.
Words that once meant boy or farm
Irritate our flesh and blood.
We are easily forgotten
By them. Could they have done better?
For there was one thing we ourselves
Could not understand:
We were native from the start,
With brown bush and the blue
Mountains, from the first moment
With wood smoke at dawn
That no one can describe, the birds,
The sticky heat we grew to love.

We thought we were exiles.
We are certainly exiles now.

The worst lie was our hope:
Perpetual tea time and the colour green.
Fantasies always suffice
But we returned to the lie:
The dirty towns, the insensitive people,
Endless tea time and the colour green.
But we can forgive this remembering
One promise: driving through
Long grass at night, the scratch
Of the grass on the truck,
And in our headlights a continent,
An Africa within. An Africa beyond.

DEVILS

That is a country where
At midday devils
Spiral from the river
And enter good Burgers
Who doze, sweating
On cast-iron beds.

Night falls. Contagion
Is complete.
The devils wind back
To the marshes,
And on the bed a thing
Sits up and scratches,
Searching for the self
It lost at noon.

I have seen a man
(The Principal Belmotto)
Write theses on a blackboard
For a whining child,
Or fill by slow amanuensis
Note-books that were logic
For his lost Empire.
And then believing he could walk
On water,
He drowned one morning
With his usual fuss,
Gurgling Aramaic
In a short, last prayer.

Another one, an Alexander,
Planned to blow the State away,
Contriving bombs
He killed his brother.
Now in a Home
He plays with paper,
And slashes foolscap into shapes
You'd swear
Could almost cry.

And lately I have seen them
In this country.
They are in the air.
Yesterday one came for me
And circled my siesta.
I laughed. Reason,
Good humour, alone
Can conquer devils.

And when from the tower
At midnight,
(Or thereafter as I choose)
I leap across the town,
The devils shall acknowledge
A superior: awed
By the heights I reach.
And I'll fly high, my friends,
Higher than the steeple,
Higher than
The priest can preach.

THE ESTUARY. AUGUST 1964

The river moves into the sea,
Waves break in the estuary:
In the tide the land goes.
From a fishing boat voices
Sound across the water
Speaking, it seems in the heat,
From the horizon, or where
The sky and sea
Are one blank thing.

At my feet the carcase
Of a monkey jumps
And roars with flies:
There are great pods
And branches from inland.
The sand flows and grinds
To sand: Africa.
The sky and sea
Are one blank thing

And once again the brave
Must suffer, through pain
Achieve a sort of freedom.
And once again the strong
Crush blindly,
Instinctively the weak
Demand each blow.
The sky and sea
Are one blank thing.

Inheritors of hate, what
Can we offer? What can atone
The weak, the strong?
Grain by grain they are
The earth we stand upon:
Silt and sand,
Detritus of the sun.
The sky and sea
Are one blank thing.

Mens' voices sound across
The water, and where I walk
The surf spreads
Leaves on the shore.
Raising glasses I bring
Waves on the river, the brown
Land closer.
The sky and sea
Are one blank thing.

THE BEACH, THE EVENING

And now the tide's way out, the sun just hot
And a wide buck nigger in blue jeans walks
The open sand. The whites glare. Black. It's not
Just colour it's his stance. He preens, he stalks.

All his body swings with nerve, with pounds
Of insolence. Slap into the waves
He bounces fully clad. And this astounds
No one. He leaps and waves his arms. He saves

Nothing. Emerges dripping, shining. Rapist!
Faker! Hopped up, slapping wet, he doubles
On the spot: then does a backward twist,
An exercise that no one sees, troubles

To see. He lopes off. Disappears. And on
The pink horizon a yacht comes up, met
By stares and tea time. All day has gone.
And now: red sails. The bloody sunset.

ASPECTS OF A FOREIGN CITY

African squalor, Latin sloth
This city has a bit of both.

Here once an empire ruled and made
These statues talk, that colonnade
A Roman crescent on the march.

Now tourists snap the crumbling arch
And eye the whores, and drink till late:
Even the sin is second rate.

THE WAR

In the City, in the heat,
They come to dawdle at the Café,
To loiter
In the rumours of the boulevard.

Two citizens sip coffee, whisper,
Calculate to a millimetre
The round of flesh a matron,
Rapacious on a gâteau,
Carries beneath her bombazine.

Red betel-lipped, compulsive, slow,
A blind, black beggar hawks
Lottery tickets.

Into the froth of his second beer,
A visitor sinks sideburns
And laps the Continental life.

Behind the *Diario* an import-
Export man adds tax and duty,
A generous cut to a special
Friend, and still comes out
With profit.

Two Paratroopers rise.
They scrape the concrete with their boots,
Then wander off and down the street,
To the North and to the West
And to the Bush: to the War
That only murmurs here:
In the City, in the heat.

NUNC DIMITTIS

It was strange what worried him –
The distorted bodies
Of people in cartoons:
Somehow the joke was lost
When a head grew fatter
Than its trunk, and it was strange
What he remembered now:
There was a farm
Where hunting birds as a boy:
    You could shoot
    Right up to the trees but there
    We left them, that
    Was their sanctuary.

He loathed past battles,
Never talked of the wars
He fought in, except
To condemn all waste. At times
He hated misery so much
He would not face it
For a son or brother,
But smiled then at servants
Or called a large black dog
To jump on the grass
Outside his window.
His strength went then.

Yet, having so much
Natural affection, it seemed
In the photograph of his mind,
A summer's evening, where
Sons and servants, jumping dogs,
Could make this moment, dying,

Much less final:
The wars were all over
And men were sane,
And the birds flew, safe,
Into the trees.

AT FORTY ODD

Alone at midday, lozenges of light
Broke loose inside the pool and down his skin
The water crackled. The sun so quick, white
Glazed the river: in that shock his twin
Flashed clear, then shivered out of sight.
They dived and met: smiling, each sank down
To clouds of cold and sand. It was like night,
Dream deep. As still as fish they lay as one.

So deep below him is that time and gone –
I see him floating, caught between two weirs,
Drifting between vague limits, losing one
And moving fast up on the other. He
Floats alone at forty odd. Does he see
His shadow swim below: the dream he fears?

A KIND OF GRASS

A kind of grass,
A kind of mountain
Have made us something.

Our words have been won
From the horizon –
So that even lies,
Our own lies,
Have reality now:

And our truth can be scratched
From a dry river bed.

II

1973 – 1979

FILIPPO ARGENTI

'Via costà con gli altri cani'

I say there are no more stars.
I say the sun has gone.
Shit covers my eyes.

I bite myself.
Doubled up, I thrash in slime.
But I remain.

And you,
You who break the light,
You who make a shadow,

Know: I never had pity for others
And here
Have none for myself.

I am Filippo.
Show me the sun.
Show me the stars.

1818. M. FRANCOIS LE VAILLANT RECALLS HIS TRAVELS TO THE INTERIOR PARTS OF AFRICA 1780–1785

I

At home in the damp hills of Champagne,
I take my warmth at the fire. Official
And unofficial birds stare glassy-eyed
From cabinets, uncurious now
And oddly meditative. As flames rise a glow
Lightens their wing feathers:
They seem to move but stand rock still.
They are not and I am not
In Africa now: yet we remain, we are
The artefacts of that long journey,
Survivors of a narrative –
A story that I chose to tell, solid
In parts, deliberately vague
In others. I had no choice, I found
A normal country, rather like paradise
In places, a garden
Camouflaged by scandal,
Darkened by a kind of history.

So from the very start, exploring,
Plume-hatted among the hordes,
I sought what had been lost and what I found
I made my own: birds, animals, a cave of leaves,
And men. My friends became the fearful tribes,
Unwanted half-breeds, and, by letters
From the wilderness
A lonely savant at the Cape. Only
The Colonists were not to be endured:
Vicious at times or just plain boring, sly –
Certainly not schooled enough
To leave the wild unploughed,

Brandy-sots who could not comprehend
Rare sensibility, true Pride.

But I was clever, had a way
Of getting what I wanted: that trick –
Of loading my fusee
With powder, wax and water
To bring a warbler down,
Immaculate
And flat on earth –
Before I broke its neck
I named the bird
And it was mine.

I had a method, yes, because I found
Buffon's stale categories a bore.
My method was to educate,
Delight, attract:
As in the breed of *Drongos*
The species multiply – *Drongri,*
Drongear, Drongo Moustache,
Drongo Fingah, and finest of them all
Disporting on a bough
Le Drongo à Raquettes.

To crawl to no god, command no slave:
This was the ordinary
Guide of my life – but given a want
Of Civility, common
To that land, good manners helped.
Narina stank of grease but liked
A buckle, most of my toys
And understood the gallantry,
The camouflage of teasing which
Hid the method. Item:
For the King of France: the Pelt

Of one Giraffe or Cameleopard –
Chased in the Canton of the Boshmen –
Beyond the Gariep.

II

So, in the end, it all went well enough.
A King and an Emperor both
Admired my great bird book.
The one has lost his head, the other
Studies seagulls on a lonely rock...
And walking in this room today
A true Apostle of Jean Jacques,
By private conversation,
Step by step, deferring, said
What I have written nicely balances
The Good with Evil, Nature with the Perfidy
Of Man.
        Is that enough, is that
What I was looking for?
I said and say again:
The Fabulous was quite destroyed
And in its place I set the Truth.
I made a country real, a normal place,
Romantic, I agree, and odd but
Savage the right way at last. I showed
There were no Giants, club-footed or one-eyed:
Who now denies that Pigmies are small men?
Monomotapa, Vigite Magna have disappeared
From the maps, and where I travelled
That continent it is not dark.
I say the best minds of the Age
Have made my Africa their own: my Truth
Feeds their Imagination. I have shown
That men in skins move in a certain
Landscape, are men like us, have names:
Confused, they love and hate.

Is that the Truth,
Is that what I see now?
There was a night, when wandering from my tent
At the stream of the Gonaquas,
I saw the moon had covered all
That forest, all the mountains with its light:
It flowed as bland as milk, the normal landscape
Seemed to shift, to alter... what I saw
Remained authentic yet I knew
It was not real.
And here much later,
Here by the fire tonight, my Africa
Is dark again. Stuffed Drongos, Trogans,
Shrikes will not flap their wings:
They sit as still as rocks. Nothing
Moves but firelight closed
In the long, high room.
The world is what it seems
Always, but it can flow beneath the moon
And change, alter the staid
Sequences of vision.
Half-blind amid
The humdrum panic of the herd,
Or camouflage of predator and prey,
I saw only what I was made to see,
Could comprehend.
Do all
Travellers into darkness know,
Their eyes half closed,
Exploring they betray themselves,
Betray what they have found?

MADAGASCAR

I am walking by the sea,
The sun is hot enough:
It warms the sand,
The wind blows along.

A black man is fishing
From a rock. The fish
At his feet are dead.
Today is not different.

A bamboo stem
Is running gripped by
A dog's jaw. The legs
Are moving.

Nothing is said as things
Are done. This is
The natural way
Things go on.

Two butterflies before me
Fly up and down –
They are gold or red.
Two or three steps
Then the wind takes them:
They drift in air and light
Toward the surf.
   It is clear
They'll never make it
To Madagascar.

THE FIRST HOURS

'...e che la mente nostra, peregrina,
più dalla carne e men da pensier presa,
alle sue visïon quasi è divina ...'

These are the first hours:
The dark is moving:

Panic in the leaves,
The voices start –
Once more the whistle, squawk:
And frantic, queer
The cry of a lourie
Robbed of a twig, or

Plaintive near the dawn,
The song of a swallow:

Banned and here –
It dips its wings
And swoops below my roof,
Casually the sky goes pink,
The sun spreads out
Its normal yellow,
Routines of the day arrange,

And sleek, insistent, full of law
A cat squats at the foot of my bed,
Obsessive as the sun that rises,
Licking and licking its paw.

ARD ROOM

his power,
ou can smell
m: the cues glitter like weapons,
the green nap of the table
was a battle ground for him where conflicts broke
in the strategy of a game.

And I remember hearing,
at night above my head,
the sound of a glass breaking and a burst
of rich laughter: then silence,
except for the powerful tread, the pacing
from angle to angle,
and the crack of a cannon
as the white slammed into the red. It's
all snuffed out now of course, like a long
Havana cigar, a Hoyo de Monterey perhaps,
smoked down for an inch or two, and never
much more. The act has gone, his gesture,
casual on an evening thirty years ago,
is obsolete: now
only a sense of ritual
pervades the room and feeds
familiar on the tokens of his power:

a German ceremonial sword,
he captured in South West, stands rigid
in a shell case: against one wall an old
propeller rots (and somewhere stuck in a drawer
there's an album showing photographs of the crash)
so that objects of steel and brass, records
of dead encounter, have made this room
a potent place, the temple of my caste

where I must pay homage, the sour pietas
of son to father, the unforgiving
love that looks for only one thing in the past:
conflict as barren as dust. I have no God
but a giant who paces above my head,
who blusters nightly that in his turn
my son shall have his saga of Fee, Fie, Fum,
to grind my bones to make his bread.

Though I stand by a half opened window
and breathe in the air,
the dust still stirs about me,
raised by a step on the floor,
and the smell that comes up is the smell of old power,
unbreaking love, unfinished war.

SPRING COMING: ZOO LAKE

I

Days like this
Before the end of winter,
Cold afternoons
When all the foreign trees
Stand bare, stand stuck to ground,
This hinterland their home,
When any shout rings brilliant
In the park – these days
Catch the senses, show things
As they are: the outlines hard,
The sounds clear.
        At five o'clock
The factory hooters howl.
Through windy streets,
Past jacarandas, London planes,
The cars come home:
Down Tyrone Avenue, Kilkenny Road,
And with them come the taxis,
Buses crammed with blacks
Who somehow here have found
Backyard rooms
To make their lives and ours.
        Last night
We heard a cold hyena whoop,
Alien, feral in the smokeless zone,
As though there were
For Africa no hope –
But down the road at Fifty-four
A senile dachshund heard him,
Yapped and soon
The suburb's dogs were barking back.
This is the echo
We never lack.

II

A time of change:
Fuzz on the willows
A child can touch –
To call it spring
Would make it seem too much,
As though we wanted
Something that's not here, not quite
The thing we're going to get.
Such longings for another season
Touch mysteries of time and place,
But momentary and slight.
        It's summer
That we long for: a green
That's moist and fat,
When contrasts blur and thicken
In the sun... big piebald days
That dawdle on the lawns,
That fleck the ponds
With deep and shallow light.
So many families come here then:
Various, multicoloured,
Free for afternoons
To wander on the paths:
The children laugh sedately,
The ribbons in their teased-out hair
Stick out and flutter as they walk:
Black families,
So well dressed,
It seems they come instinctively
To act a dream of middle class,
And here they find it,
Warm and modest,
Gentle by the Lake.

III

But now
Cold afternoons
And wind along the streets:
Crates of empties pile
And crash upon the pavement
Outside the bottle store.
Half-drunk, black workers
Curse all passers-by.
Somewhere beyond the shops,
Metallic and monotonous
A burglar siren starts,
It rises to crescendo, falls
Away, then starts again
To howl across the sky.
Another false alarm,
Or is it real this time?
The noise persists
And will not fade
Or falter in the weakening light:
As cars come home
And buses fill the streets.
Above the bluegum tops
The sun begins to sink.
Held for seconds in a branch,
It glows like fruit
Then drops below the houses.
In sudden dusk
Lights jump at the fountain,
Gloss the trees: light covers
The darkness of
This urban,
Artificial lake.

THE FIRST DANGER

With the first danger we gave ourselves
Another name. We made
Less noise in the evenings
And used dry fuel for the fires,
Though by then it was known where we lived.

Threatened again, we changed our language
Entirely, using the tongue our neighbours spoke.
Alert, we moved our fields
After the first sowing. From then on there could be
No ceremony of the first fruits.

We lay silent in the forest,
Not sure what we would surprise. It seemed, turning,
The path would ambush us. How could we kill
If we did not know the hunted? To disembowel
The unknown would be wrong. It could die wrongly, being

A thing not to be played with, touched: as
Above so below.
But when it did not rain we knew
That we were lost, and knew
We could not speak our own language.

We had forgotten the songs and how to dance
The old way: the slow revolving steps,
The rites of coupling. What we ate
Was raw or half-charred: the meat
And pelt and gut of rats.

We had ambushed the shadows,
Stuck knives into the shade of ourselves.
A threat was not caring: power was
Lightning that bloomed on the horizon,
A fire that left us arid, untouched.

GRAMMAR

Slowly no sound but the sound of rain,
The calmness of it falling deep
Into the night.

Somewhere outside they break a man's face
Slowly. Now the face has no eyes,
No country. The tongue
Is pulled out: I must speak.
These words are my own,
The memory.

I am blind deep into the night,
Remember a country where rain
Blurs on the window and slowly
A fire chokes on its ash,
And there is grammar:
Sounds that were made before.

Broken.
Somewhere outside the night goes on,
Slowly the rain etcetera.

ON THE WILD COAST

On the wild coast the cattle
come down to the sea after grazing.
They lie in the sand together, staring:
the sea comes in and goes out.

They walk away at the cool
of evening, slow to the top
of the dunes then bellow and kick
down the other side homewards

for milking: and darker
they move through the smoke and they stop
at the houses. The voices
are loud and then soft:

women talking to children,
the murmur of men at the fires.

SEPTEMBER AT THE TUILERIES

Blond waterfalls of sunlight in the fountain
or *déjà vu* that lurks around the corner:

If I have no appointments or
old dates to keep it is
because I'm satisfied with what lies right
before me, with all that's here,
so solid, blatant and replete,
or so I like to think.

These monuments of grandeur:
winged Victories, granite Despairs,
bulky philosophers immarbled forever,
these statues of the naked Gods all hold
their own dumb rhetoric, are myths
or portents made to stroll by,
chipped precisely for such morning promenades –
and yet I'm worried by a lack of plausibility.
Such postures call for gravitas
and I am not condign:
the statuary's become banal,
quotidian as the ice cream vans
whose awnings stripe the Allées.

Around and through the gardens go
the people who are not at home
beneath such regal, elderly trees:
almost with envy, covertly they glance
at those who go about
their business here: the ones
in overalls, who clear the debris,
indifferently belonging, demanded
by something more important than themselves:
authorities of paper, trash, the leaves.

Observe I do not play the *faux-naïf*
Septembering in Paris.
I sit upon this iron bench and do not find,
pretend to find, a marble Grace
anything but foolish.
No appointments please: I am absolutely modern,
intact and not quite bored. I blink
while pigeons flap around my knees
or peck about my feet
in simulating, stagey jerks: bad actors –
idle, corpulent birds strutting
as if they wore court hose – and yet
I must suppose their ancestors
once fluttered here and shed
democracies of waste on white perruques,
on Montesquieu with *Persian Letters*
or Gautier chiselling verses in his head.
Or this is what I think.

But I am meeting no one here,
have no slow revenants to greet
with skins as red as steak tartare,
no ghost to conjure squeaking from a fountain:
I am glad to have the statues as they are,
upon their pedestals and streaked with white –
and mute. Just that
and all is right.

Thus not to play as God a little
is best and safest. I'm on vacation:
I am here from other business, other places.
So let the fountain rise in due serenity,
its babble only be a late September,
foreign sound. The square is quiet with heat:
I make it so. I disconnect, I close my eyes,
relieve the present of its tumult, ban

its noise. I wait for Rimbaud,
he the least intact, who was in hell.
And absolutely modern, of course I know
just round that dazzled corner stand
the breath-filled bodies of the sacred dead.

THE MEDITERRANEAN IDIOT SOMNAMBULATES

Benign at evening the Cathedral
purrs with prayer,
through open doors Jehovah throbs
across the darkening square.

The lights blink badly at the Café Luxe:
Zerlina hums.
She wantons with her pearly teeth
on Juan's flesh. He comes.

The Gendarme thinks. His uniform distaste
(all that he knows)
has put black warts on his fingers,
hard red corns on his toes.

The young men at the fountain, broken, wear
old coats like capes –
their words and what they feel are lost.
Worn-out, the Triton gapes.

Around the hotel bins a raunchy sow
grunts Pig and snaps,
snuffles for a kind of virtue:
the waste of tourist traps.

There's nothing but nonsense at the window:
dry pantyhose
flicks endless goodbye to the night.
A blue moth comes and goes.

Now church-mice muddle in the brazen doors,
they feel the light,
rustle to holes across the town:
the wind goes out of sight.

And out of touch, of moth, of pig and mice,
the idiot calls:
climbing the staircase his madness
slobbers above him, it growls

and sends him through fragilities of dark
to hunt, alone,
the phantasies of God asleep,
whose dreams turn men to stone.

PREHISTORY, CATEMBE FERRY.

Prawn-juice, sweat,
blood-bright piri-piri –
flies loop and wobble,
land upon the bread.

        Fly high
Old Fly, we're canned
on vinho verde.
And someone said:

One of the crew fell over,
got chopped in the propeller.

        Hazy, LM city
floats across the bay:
balloons and pops. The ferry grinds
toward the khaki shore.

They're always pissed on payday.

        Stand. Up now.
Cackle. Belch. Tip to cuddle and
helping hand. We'll make it
to the jetty:

They're drunk, I tell you,
the whole weekend.

        And from the deck
we see it floating,
face down, dipping
in tepid water.
Lights out, dead drunk,
it leaks pink blood and,
as the ferry goes forever,
rolls against our backwash.

GRAND HOTEL

I

Younger than those around him,
his hands
are as pale as Riesling.
We are told he is in Fabrics:
'Designing', he says.
        But why
will he not sit down?
And when will he stop talking,
so well, so knowledgeably about
the etchings of Picasso:
or is he now
on food and wine?
        Why ask?
There's more to come.
We are to hear about
the bitter squabble
he's having this instant
with his 'darling, irrational,
fizzpop of a mum'.

II

Her eyes stare
from a whirlpool of wrinkles.
She likes it to be said
they are blue, blue
as the violets in Spring.

Now she will show her water-colours,
painted on soft paper,
pale washes of pink or rose that fade
eluctably into
mutations of celadon.

The smallest sell for Twenty Pounds,
(she has trouble with the currency)
but if she likes you,
something she at once *feels*,
she'll let them go
for nearer Twelve.

Oh why,
ambushed at morning tea,
did I smile at her? Why
was I brought up
to be nice to old ladies,
never taught to evade
their petal-blue, glinting,
money-mad eyes?

MKULU KAKHULU

I

The men of the Northern Province are troubled.
Their hearts are heavy. They have come to see me.

Like all people of that region they are fools, these men,
But they have learned how to cower. They do this correctly.
They know the way to my heart is in the obedience:
That is why they call me Father and kiss my feet.

I give them permission to speak.

'O Mkulu Kakhulu, Life President,
The hearts of your people are heavy.
We, your children of the North, suffer.
We suffer because there is no Development there.
Unlike your children of the South
We have no Infrastructure, there are no factories
For making beer or bread, O Father,
There is no Cash Economy where we come from'.

II

Some say I have no heart.
Some say I have lost all feeling.
Let those who say that know
I was touched by the sorrow of these people.

I decided to help the Northern Province.

'My children, go back to your huts in the bush.
Go back and celebrate, for I,
The Mkulu Kakhulu, Life President,
Have decided to give you Development:
I shall show how I love my people.

First, a road of tar will go from my Capital
Straight to a place I shall choose in the North:
And there on a hill I shall build

A shining Palace, a symbol of my love,
My respect for those who live in the North.
It shall cost at least Ten Million Freedoms,
To furnish it will take another Six.

Let it be told in the villages how I pander to my people –
All the bedrooms will be en suite and have telephones,
The swimming pool will be Olympic size,
The bathrooms in marble will have gold taps,
The small private cinema will charm my foreign guests,
And the barracks, tastefully disguised as servant quarters,
Will house a full battalion of Para-Military Police.

Then, every year in Autumn
When the Northern Province is just tolerable after the rains,
I shall come on a State Visit.
I shall come for about three days
And thus my people shall know
The Mkulu Kakhulu, Life President,
Thinks of you, cares for his children,
Even those of the North'.

III

Backwards, upon all fours,
They have crept from my Presence.
They have made their songs of praise,
Clapping and ululating for a full hour,
Because that is how these savages celebrate.

It is good I have solved their problem.
Their gratitude is touching, excessive perhaps,
(They never know when to stop)
But what did they expect when they came to me?
I am generous, always, to beggars.

But the way their minds work continues to puzzle me.
At times like these I always wonder:
Do my people truly understand me?

WE ALWAYS GREET YOU SMILING

We always greet you smiling,
Raising a hand as you drive past –
And should you wish, we pose before our huts,
Set among dry mealie stalks,
The rolling hills of dusty veld.
        Sometimes,
Unasked, the piccanins will sing and dance
(You always like that part), and certainly
A few cents help.
        But have you seen
How joyfully we starve our dogs,
How hopelessly we beat our women?
        And do you know
That when their hungry bellies swell
We hate our children?

We want to learn from you.
We always greet you smiling.

THE OLD LOCATION

And here as well.
First a memory,
Then in the red road's
Dust the old location:

Peach blossom
Deep in the houses,
Trees like big
Pink flowers

Bursting out
From yards, the mad
Umbrellas stuck
Cockeyed, absurd

On rubbish heaps:
As if there'd been
A freedom overnight,
Hope breaking

Out above
The walls of mud,
The bending tin,
Flowering

To celebrate.
And then I pass
And for that second, just,
One looks at me.

She looks at me
And washes
Small rags and denim:
And in her eyes she holds

The frailty of blossom,
And deeper,
The old location
That does not change.

NOT OFTEN

Not often a night as good as this:
    below the house
the mountain moves in cloud, above
    the sky is full of stars.

Five miles away across the valley
    lights come on and we, by love outcast,
smile
    at such unearthly peace.

Wind stirs again, rattles in the dark,
    it moves about the house:
it loiters, whining. Deep within
    the miles of night

we hear it coming, its breath
    is on our breath, our life:
again the loss and wanting,
    mortal disquiet.

JOHANNESBURG NOVEMBER

The winter gone in hate.
    The summer.
Invisible in sunlight,
tongues of flame
    crawl the street.

Maddening, the city swelters,
the suburbs deep in roses,
    jacarandas.
The hovels and high-rises steam,
    squat,
as old as ovens, bread,
    as old
as smoke and ashes,
    sweat.

And somewhere in the city
    you are waiting:
your eyes are grey, they see
    the smoke and ashes.
You madden in the heat.
    I write of you.
I touch you in the city.

Dogs shamble in the yard,
fly blatant at what passes.
    This is rage.
So: falling back, sequestered,
they crouch among the flowers.

The stink of blossom. Wind,
    sour,
comes breathing into lives.
    Pours off.
It pours across the maps
and these are streets.

I touch you in my life, the city.

Giving and taking, nothing and glut,
    it is older than itself.
Fattening, it squats upon itself
    in flames that burn
invisible in sunlight: streets
    on fire where a child's hand,
black, a fist is raised against the flowers,
    dog-nosed, the blatant
    glut and sweat.

I touch you in the heat.

Doors opening and closing.
    Contracts, bread.

The jacarandas squat and flower.
The wasted petals, purple
    on the street,
    explode and stink.
The wind is hot. An oven.

Giving and taking, all was here,
    here in the coming.
It was human. It was bread.
    They crouch among the roses.

I touch my sweat. A concentration.
I live within the city in my love.
    I touch you now:
the wind is in your eyes, the flame
    that crawls the street,
    the blossom.

The city is my life and you are in it.

III

Versions
1974 – 1994

THE AGE

From the Russian of Osip Mandelstam

This age, my beast:
Who can stare into the centre of your eye,
Whose blood will mend the broken back
Of two long centuries? Blood the creator
Flows from the throat of the earth –
On the threshold of this new day
The parasites are crawling in the fur of your back.

My beast must drag its backbone to its death:
The waves break against its vertebrae.
Again, again
The lamb is taken, the crown of its head,
The tender fontanelle, is crushed
And there is blood on the earth:
At sunrise, the sacrifice.

Life must be dragged from its captivity:
A new world must begin,
The tangled days must be unravelled
To the sound of the wind.
Man's horror rocks the age, beats like the breakers
On its spine – and in the bush a serpent dreams
Its own gilt rhythms.

And once again the buds will swell,
Green tips push forth, but your back is broken,
My lovely, disconsolate age.
Cruel and weak,
With a mindless smile, you turn your head
Back like a beast that once pulsed with life
And stare, stare at the tracks of your feet.

EASTER TRANSIT
Steinkopf 1983
From the Afrikaans of Phil du Plessis

The flanks
of these dire hills
bloom
wax-green.

Do they speak
of atonement,
of death,
of fragrant Spring
and blossom
on the hyssop,
do they speak
of another
Autumn?

On this journey
I go in the night,
into the night
while a dry wind
escorts the moon
and me,
and roughens
the ridges.

Ahead on the road
the slaughterhouse truck:
and I
smell wool and dung and blood.

TWO MARES

From the Provençal of Le Comte Guilhem de Poitiers

I have two mares and both are good,
    Under my knees
They canter well. It has been said
    I mount the best in the land.

    My strawberry Roan
Comes from the mountain, and she has all
    The wildness of that breed.
    She bucks and prances,
    Shies backstep,
But when she feels my fingers in her neck,
Her flank, all fear is gone, her eyes
Are soft: trembling, she nuzzles
    The parsnip in my hand.

    How different now
My Golden Bay: she comes from level pastures,
    She has that order in her beauty.
    I knew her as a foal
    And even then adored her.
How I cursed the day she went,
Sold to another master. But now
She's mine again, I ride her as I will,
    Whatever the legalities are.

My charming mares! At evening
    When I cross the field
Each greets me with such grace:
    The Roan will stamp
And toss her mane,
    The Bay will whicker
Soft as purring. Ah yes... apart
    They are so gentle, lively

To my touch, but that, my friends,
Is where the sweetness stops.
    Just put them side by side,
Just lead them out together and then watch
    All hell break loose...
Buck and snort and bite: you'd think
    They'd seen a stallion!
They even turn on me, so help me God.
At times I think they'd both be glad
    To break my heart.

Now tell me friends, what shall I do?
    Help me in my doubt.
It's clear that one of them must go:
    But which? How can I
    Live without
Joy that is wild, as high as the mountain,
    Or pleasure that's rich,
    As deep as the plain?

A GOD UNKNOWN

From the Italian of Dante Alighieri

Giant horn of flame
in black of hell
that stooped and flickered,
murmuring, and as
wind took it
jumped erect and roared
in speech, a tongue
of fire that flickered
in eternity, speaking
these words:

I

Caught by a woman's art
I lived that year,
that year or more
upon her island,
held in her arms,
bewitched by art,
held by flesh until,
sated, one dawn I woke
and launched my ship
upon the deep, set out
upon my journey, cleaving
the wine-black sea.

Nothing could hold me back,
nothing could stop me:
no thought of family –
wife, father, child –
could draw me home.
There was
only the power within me,
the spirit

driving forward, a greed
to know the world –
all evil, yes, and all
the good of Man.

And so we went:
one ship alone
and those few men
who never left me:
and sailed out through
that Middle Sea:
saw countries, islands
floating past –
Sardinia went, Morocco,
until our ship
reached Spain at last.

II

We were old men now, slowing
with age, as we came
to that narrow strait
where a god
has set his sign:
pillars of rock
that men should go
no further. But I
sailed onward, passing
Seville upon my right,
while to the left
Africa began
to drop from sight.

And here I spoke
these words to my men:
'Brothers, you
who never doubted,

who stood with me,
faced danger times
beyond your counting,
Look ahead now, look,
for we have reached
the West. Give me
what little time
we still have left
to honour life,
to be the first
to look upon
a land without people,
the first to see,
the first to know
a world
beyond the sun.

Think of the seed
from which you have come:
you were not made
to live like brutes
but to follow
that spirit within you,
to face
whatever waits ahead
with what you know,
with what you are,
accepting
whatever you will find
with courage'.

III

Few words: but I
could not hold my men,
even had I wanted – so
swung the ship,

stern to the dawn
and prow to the west.
Then in our hands the oars
began to beat like wings,
taking mad flight –
our course was now
forever to the south.

At night we began to see
new stars glittering
around that other pole:
and our own star,
our North,
had sunk so low,
it never rose above
that ocean's floor.

Five times the light
beneath the moon
blazed out:
five times went black
since we had first
started our great journey,
when finally a mountain,
blurred by distance,
floated before us,
but higher than any
I had seen before.

IV

And we were glad,
each man among us,
but soon our joy
was turned to grief
as from the New Land,
suddenly,

a storm arose and struck
the ship three times,
spinning it round
and all the water
turning with it:
the fourth strike
hit the stern, pushing
it high, the prow
sliding under
as though pulled
from below.

It seemed,
as the water
closed above us,
a god unknown,
some other being,
had willed our fate
and at this place,
and at this time,
had planned our end.

AT THE CAFE SAN MARCO

From the Italian of Eugenio Montale

My Swiss chronometer had the bad habit
of deciding for itself what time it was.
That is why
when I came to seat myself at the café
it was 5 o'clock and not 6.
Getting there early was unimportant perhaps
or even a stroke of good luck –
but postponement, the waiting
had been hard on her too
and when we met
we were both as pale as each other.
    When it comes to the final
(or so you think) parting
how long should it take?
No sex manual I've ever seen
gives illustrations of love dying,
the passing of a god.
When such events occur
whether a watch is fast or slow
counts for nothing.

SUCCULENTS

From the Italian of Eugenio Montale

A distant relative of mine collected succulents:
people from all around came to see them.
Even that dilettante of prosaic verse,
the famous (?) de Lollis came.
They were both well known at the Monterosa,
a restaurant, long since gone, for single men;
and today the hot-houses, the succulents, the visitors,
even the garden where these marvels were on show,
no longer exist. As for my relative, well,
it's as though he'd never been on earth.
    At one time he studied at Zurich
and failed every subject. But when things in this country
took a turn for the worse, he'd shake his head and say
'Ah Zurich, Zurich...'

I don't know if a sense of the absurd
has any meaning in the all or nothing
of our life but to have one
certainly helps.

BEING CAREFUL

From the Italian of Eugenio Montale

They were not wrong, warning me,
to take a long spoon
each time I supped with the Devil.

Unfortunately, however,
on those rare occasions
only a short one was available.

QUARTET

From the Italian of Eugenio Montale

In a yellowing snapshot,
taken forty years ago,
fished out from the bottom of a drawer –
your face, grave in its sweetness,
and I, your servant, am beside you.
Behind us is Sbarbaro, the poet
who studied mosses, and Elena Vivante,
the queen of us all. We're here to watch
four hacks, whipped bloody
in a shell-shaped square
and the crowd is going mad.
        But the time?
I said it was forty years ago
though that means nothing:
I don't believe in time, the big bang,
or anything that measures events
by starts and finishes. I do believe
a quality of being, an essence
is held in something, in someone.
On that day that someone was you.
But how did it happen and for how long?
And again the detestable notion
of time recurs.

A VISITANT

From the Italian of Eugenio Montale

Whenever my aunt from *Pietrasanta*
appeared at the end of the avenue,
we boys made a rush for the attic:
we had to get away from her.
   She was old and boring:
that was her sin but to the young,
even then, it seemed a crime,
quite beyond comprehension,
an insult.
   My father would embrace her and listen
to the river of misfortune in which
the old woman swam like a fish;
and he would slip a couple of coins
into her open bag. Finally
he would say, 'Quick, off with you now
or you'll miss your train.'
(She always travelled the cheapest class).
   I never saw her really.
Today she'd be over a hundred: but,
whenever I read or hear the name *Pietrasanta,*
I think of those few coins and of being poor:
I think of the grief in the world
and the fortune / misfortune of having ancestors,
of being the posterity, three times removed,
of God knows who, of someone perhaps
who never really lived.

I DON'T KNOW IF GOD...

From the Italian of Eugenio Montale

I don't know if God ever realized
that the vast machine he'd made
had a basic error, that there was in fact
a miscalculation
at the heart of the universe.
I mean, look how long it took to build
and how quickly it destroyed itself.
There must have been something wrong
right at the beginning:
disaster happened and then
there was emptiness again. No,
I don't think he ever realized.

IN THE GARDEN

(From the Italian of Eugenio Montale)

You walk down the grand avenue –
a sky blue with summer
hovers above and, as you arrive,
a cloud, linen-white,
cools the dog-day heat.

We sit at the same old garden bench.
Then, all at once, a puff of wind
and your straw-hat starts to blow off:
you stand to grab it and so
once more you sit beside me.

The wings of the great sea-pine
are like sails that open
to tear us away, beating against
the wind from the shore, bearing us up
and along this coast

and, in a duet of names and memories,
will reach in one great final tack
the haven of Genoa. But the sun
is setting already. Slant rays
lengthen its splendour: they

vanish and return. The memory
of other evenings such as this
doubles and redoubles our horizon.
Unforgotten from older days,
fugitive, the moment itself is here.

Now the wind has dropped as well.

WIND ON THE HALF-MOON

From the Italian of Eugenio Montale

That was not the way to you,
crossing the great bridge:
had you wished it I would have come,
navigating drains and sewers:
but the sun flashed on the verandah windows
and by then I had lost my strength.

'Tell me,' said the man preaching on the crescent,
'do you know where God is?'
I knew so I told him.
He shook his head and went on the wind that rushed,
that lifted men and houses into the sky,
into the blackness of pitch.

THE LETTER UNWRITTEN

From the Italian of Eugenio Montale

A vision first of dolphins:
the children playing upon their backs,
the fish rippling two by two,
and the sunrise swarming again and again,
and the hours threaded, one upon the other,
days joining the necklace of time –
is this what you wanted,
is this what you want?
                                        Better far
never to have heard of you,
never to have seen
the brilliance beneath your lids.
It is different here on earth.

I cannot go,
I cannot turn my face again to you.
The evenings spread:
night will not end –
it burns like a scarlet forge
and prayer is torture.
                                        Even now
the bottle cast upon the sea
has not reached you: it floats
in surges of water and rock. The waves
break and are empty, the surf uncurls
at the end of the earth.

THE HOUSE ON THE FRONTIER

From the Italian of Eugenio Montale

Forget. You have forgotten
that house on the frontier,
the cliff that waits for you,
desolate, sheer above rocks.
You do not remember
the night your thoughts
swarmed about the house,
immortal, uneasy.

For years a gale has lashed the walls.
When you laugh you are unhappy.
For no reason the compass
swings crazily. You cannot guess
what way the dice will fall.
You have forgotten. Another time
distracts your memory. The thread
winds round and I...

I hold one end, but the house
goes back and back and the cock
on the roof is dark with smoke:
it spins and has no pity.
I hold one end
but you are alone.
At night I cannot hear
the sound of your breathing.

Yes, here is the horizon –
and once or twice I have seen
the lights of a passing tanker.
Is this where we cross? (And always
the breakers that swarm on the rocks,

the crumbling away.) You
do not remember the house, all night
it has been my own.

I do not know who has entered it
or who it is that has left.

IV

1980 – 1994

TO HAVE LOVE

To have love and then lose it:
the white hail in the orchard
lying with leaves it has stripped
and the storm moving away.

A DREAM OF GUESTS

I

When the year came to my broken house
the guests were there bringing their own guests.
They had the long face and poor digestion
of those who had once been rich.
And what was there to eat but sour bread,
and wine as thick and black as mud?

Away from this house with its smell of the unwashed
over the blue sea to their islands,
long since gone my children, leaving no toys
but the doll at the foot of my bed,
the arm torn off, eyes out, its belly gutless:
and this I tell all comers is my wife, long dead.

II

We waste his land and sell his gilded tomes:
his colony of schoolbooks – wordlists and Latin primers
being most in demand. In this house
we all have the same odd pace, the witty eyes
of those who have the death-wish. It is a broken place
and we would like to leave these passages,
derelict with ancient rubbish, modern rage.

No one believes there are harlots in the attic
ready to satisfy our one inane desire –
no one believes there are golden-long vintages
brooding in the cellar.

There are no facts that matter here,
only absurd alcoves reached by a rickety stair,
or porticoes stuffed with sofas piled
to form a hopeless barrier on the way
to flea-infested granaries, not filled.

Swooping at twilight,
we have seen no swallows in the courtyard,
but have observed
other things wounded, broken-backed in the gutter.

III

But with such a host there is no going.
The guests must stay and listen, crossing their legs,
yawning, bored numb by his soliloquies
on travel and the pleasures of a well-stocked mind.
They will hear his rant, his explicable loathing of Pygmies,
again and again. Until he dies they will continue to exploit
his miserable possessions and burn his ancient gifts.
And in the half-shuttered light of the long afternoon
they must listen as he turns to them, defensive and accusing:
as by revenge in a mirror they will watch him step,
pace odd, alive, and the staring back
of witty, death-searching eyes.

AGAIN

Again
we lie together:
holding hands
we talk of being children,
knowing we have come to where
our lives begin
and where our lives must end.

Falling into sleep
I cannot move. Cradled
in that ancient mud,
the primal shore, I know
that there is danger.

And I am not alone:
once more
two fish lie in that dream,
alive and out of water, both
just breathing.

GRAMARY

It is the children in the dusk:
are not what were:
bone and spirit.

Where I am I do not know
and where I go to I
cannot see.

It was the children playing
in the dusk,
(not this dusk) those

other children, not us and now.
Under the trees enormous
the voices seek and hide,

seek and hide.
Known is this:
my only known,

and it is gone.

A full moon
blinds the sky.

THE DUST IN THE WIND

The grass black and a turbulence,
a blossoming
that shakes from the plum tree
clockwise,
that drops a hundred yards away.

Spring comes with its mortal odours,
a flicker of red in the hills at night,
and age is a taste, dry on the tongue:
all day
there is dust in the wind.

THE FIRST, FAR BEAT

In the mountains
the first, far beat
of spring thunder:

thick with young,
a lizard on the rock
moves its head

and in the flank
the quick heart pulses.

HOMAGE TO DAVID LIVINGSTONE
PHAKAMILE YALI-MANISA

It has always been a little hard
to make it move, to get the drama.
Yet when Bellini drew a saint
receiving the stigmata
he filled the open spaces
with dogs and hares he copied
from a pattern book.
He knew a miracle
could hold that vulgar stock.

Mendelssohn in his symphony,
The Reformation,
finds tunes abundant
in the common store:
he makes a solemn gala throb
with lieder from the street,
and turns to Luther,
converting
A Mighty Fortress Is Our God.

Now hear Manisi in his praising:
the words that circle words,
you have the skill, Imbongi,
and yet this tongue
I hardly understand.
I say you do
but do not make your song:
your poem calls back –
it is

and is not memory. Your words
beat time, they drum
and circle round each other:
as dancers do who clap to start
and hold a rhythm, known at once
and new. Here is life's rhetoric,
a shape that hovers in the song –
and when it vanishes,
it must be there.

SORRY, DOUGLAS

On first hearing that, in a newspaper interview about his poetry, Douglas Livingstone had refused to discuss why his poems did not directly address 'the struggle'.

Sorry, Douglas, you're out of fashion,
unversed in the prosody of shit:
your poems are only born of passion –
revealing, merely, your radiant wit.

SIR TOM

No longer seen at office or the club, he was 'retired':
flailing around his Randlord house each day he'd
light his high Victorian lamps in every room
to search for mambas, or he'd plead

for 'sweeties' from his own black cook, who shyly wept
to see his master so demeaned. He'd slaver
at his neighbour's fence and shout that there were diamonds
in his rockery. With children he was meant to have a

special kind of sympathy. I was his favourite,
so my parents said, and when we went to luncheon
once a month on Sunday, they'd place me on a high stool
next to 'Father'. He'd say the grace, then punch upon

the table, shout 'my sweet boy' and squeeze my puny chin
with his gross hand, while all around us aunts
and uncles kept on smiling: awkward, docile, prim, as course
would follow course, borne by servants

older than Igoli. They'd dodder on from place to place
with plates of sugared pumpkin, beans or yellow rice. All style,
all energy was broken in that room, the curtains drawn
against the post-noon sun. Talk would last a while

then hush down to a silent, sated calm, so all you'd hear
would be the clink of knife and fork against the plate
as close on twenty people waited till it took
the old man's wit to start again, to speak. It was my fate

that one such afternoon he turned to me and asked:
'What would you like, my darling boy?' Without thinking,
I said I wanted toast. So toast was brought. It came
on its own dish and in a silver rack. The old man winking

to the table – for all his children and their children
had paused and now were watching – took off the covering
napkin, drew out a piece and lavished it in butter,
nimbly slicing off the crusts. Hovering

behind us I heard Jim, the oldest servant there,
just barely whisper 'shame', though why he said this I
did not understand quite then. A square of soft, warm
butter-sodden toast filled the middle of the plate. 'Why,

close your eyes, my boy', the old man said, 'Open
wide!' I made my lips into an O, smiling to the giver.
Eyes shut, I turned towards grandfather,
trusting. Into my throat he jabbed a long coarse sliver

from the crust. It rasped and burnt my skin. I gagged
in panic and could not scream while still he stabbed and bent
it down into my throat. Some uncle (or my father, was it?)
pulled him gently off. Choked with shock, I was quickly sent

or carried from the dining room and put upon
a couch in the small parlour. At the table old Sir Tom
stared at his family. Rightly, they had always known
children never should presume or, if they did, learn that from

such babies must come men. But strangely, now, the old man broke,
gasping into tears. He said he saw white skulls and not
their cosy, smiling faces. Blue-eyed, haggard, he too was led
sobbing from the table. Perhaps, at last, he'd understood

how sick he was and old, hearing Doom's blatancy:
the awful nonsense raving, Hell seething in his head.

THAT

I

I am
astonished at the subtleties
of green, of colour
this year brings.

God knows,
standing on this hill,
there are shades
I cannot name, words
not found. I can say only
the trees are somewhat dark,
the vines a lighter
green, that God
stands for what
I do not know and cannot
apprehend: faith
become a pinch of air, the gap
between my thumb
and index finger, out
of all this light
one millimetre: sensing
that high trust
as if it were
an uncontrollable fit
of sneezing which
does not happen often in
the busyness, the smallness
of a life.

II

I feed,
feed on the green
and try to name
the rich vocabulary

of tones, to touch
long glossaries
of colour.

Once I saw
a cobra rise and heard
it click among
these vines: a picture then
of fury in a garden.
It oddly seemed
to satisfy a need
for simple, consonant,
symbolic things,
a killer swaying
under buds of grape,
until its mottle
coils were lost
within the green, forgotten
till I need
a serpent in my mind,
another millimetre.

III

Speak! I say,
and in the evening
The Lord walked
in the garden and
there was that
business
of a man, a woman
and some fruit,
not to mention snake
that coils between
thought and sense,
that clicks along
the vine of memory.

If only seeing,
seeing this,
was all believing:

there is no burning bush
unless it burn, green
within my mind, green
within my naming,
unconsumed.

IV

In truth I know.
I know The Lord
did speak as He
speaks always:
I hear because
I am
as unconvinced,
as diffident
as Moses hearing
riddles in
a wilderness:

I am,
He says,
I am that
I am.

THE BESTIARY

Awake,
we all have masks for this –
but the dream's a bestiary:
asleep, we comprehend
animals suddenly.

THE SHELL

Simple, I hold it to my ear
and it roars
with complication.

Now, on the table
it is dumb: agog
with the irony of the ocean.

THE TEXT

A story at first made up
by a mother for her child.
The cook heard it,
brewing a broth, and the next thing
it was scuttling round the market,
a small but growing larger
uncatchable rat.
Some years later (3 to 900)
The Fable Man was hunting
and put it in his bag
and everywhere the children heard it
(again and please again).

Soon, quite soon, it
began to sing and dance
moon upon moon upon moon –
it had clothes in its cupboard
and puns up its sleeve,
at least six hats and
not all of them funny.
Some said when it laughed
it was crying
but most said it was
the other way round.

Wise men and things began
to hang around it,
to hang upon it, to make
their lives from it,
its wizening. O
and it grew so very old –
its nose was in its chin,
the eyes fed-up and weepy.
The stomach rumbled,

the brain forgot to remember
almost everything except
that once it had been told
to a child. Then it knew,
at last, it had died.

THE ASTROLOGER

Look! I have a drink in my hand
and the afternoon to lean against.

I possess nothing.

My thoughts possess me.
All day I have worked
on columns of prediction
that will colour the life
of a housewife over the hill.

I assume she is the Gemini
who will meet a stranger
and find happiness
after a quarrel.

She will be
a little short of money
but truly astonished
by the stranger.

Go well my thoughts
I do not possess you.

Ah! And as the light goes
starlings whistle from the gutter.

Abracadabra!

And now the evening star.

HONEY

And the quarrel
and the mess:
bees deep in their hive,
deep in their honey.

LAURA

'e veggiola passar si dolce e ria'

Laura shows me the loaf she has made
crusted with seed.
It is warm like sweat, she says.

Laura plays chess and takes men to bed.

She holds the loaf in both her hands,
with womanly care. It is,
as it were, the head
of a child, some boy hot
with a fever.

THE BOWL OF TULIPS

'And the bowl of tulips', you said,
'look how demure they stand,
little women in scarlet cloaks.'

And I thought of red-riding-hood
and the wolf's tongue and your lips,
your red and secret lips.

THE ABANDONED FARM

Like two unbroken animals
that will not eat or rest,
we struggle with our love. Outside,
upon the stoep the toy windmill
spins and jerks its blades: tinny,
they clack and creak and may not pause
under the south-wester.

Now the wheat is tawny, rustling
at noon and ripe: beyond, mountains
loom out blue: khaki-dark, the river
loops and lingers out of sight.
The milk comes thick from the cow.
Around the eaves the swallows whirr
and chatter late into the night.

And we are animals of love:
restless we play and butt upon
our mattress, taut and naked we
assume the grace of time and know
it now, not then, not later:
this joy that comes beyond the past
and long before the future.

THE MAP

Dropped, dropped naked by the fire
we move toward ourselves,
mouth upon mouth, astride
the wane and wax of light,
dropped to each other, moving,
as in that map we saw
a green cartouche of negroes,
bandanna'd in their legend,
Azanian rivers, and when
a dolphin plumed in air
we moved amongst
old dhotied hindoos,
east upon east,
the caravels beyond us,
sails against firelight,
time upon time, this deep
sobriety of pleasure,
moving, as when
a good breeze rills across the harbour
and all the waves are slow,
the journey maps its end:
the sails are furled on caravels
and we make landfall slowly,
coasting in on firelight.

VENICE

You will know how quiet it is:
under water, under air,
the colonnades are hushed,
the great piazza silent:
and you will know
the dream below a dream,
the city drowning,
the palaces that wince together,
kneeling
where plague is light,
where swallows loop
in fluent air,
painting with their flight
the domes of churches.

And gone
the blood and spirit
when
a movement of the fingers made
a whore in sullen light
playing with two dogs,
one fierce, one coy:
sated with ennui,
she scarcely probes
the potent rabies of the heart,
or smugness in the flesh of things,
and yet forever is.

And turning you will see yourself,
will understand
the juggler in the square
who points to that slow place
where some great city drowns,
a sleight of hand
below the surface.

Take and you are taken.
Dream now and kneel
under the quiet horizon.

NATIVITY

If there is a prince in this picture
it is the child in the arms of its mother,
simple and naked with power.

The kings know this and kneel,
bestowing their glamour,
breathless with knowledge.

Behind is the dawn and a smell of honey:
little farms, towers,
an artefact of country,

a fable that wanders
through olive and vine,
an earth that is pale and then tawny.

Sun breaks in the hills and, startled, the light
runs like a lizard to the sky.
The mother stares at God.
She does not know she is smiling.

MIMESIS

All afternoon across the next-door garden
two men are calling to each other,
imitating birds (first the doves).
I am recuperating. One of them,
I imagine from the sound, is raking leaves
while the other
clips an ornamental shrub or rosebush.
        I narcotise myself in sun,
absorbing all the bubble of their noise,
the cooing, whistle and odd chirrups,
and cannot tell what man is bird
or bird is man, only that here is life,
a casual, pleasing thing
that takes its quality from wit.
Lazily, I glory in the noise,
half-smiling fall asleep
or fall into a hush or daydream
where all at once there is no sound,
a silence so acute the garden quivers.

        Intensive Care:
I woke one night and saw a man
explode with death, a snorting arch of agony:
around his bed the nurses
tried to beat him back to life.
There was such silence in the ward,
blue neon-lit:
drugged, I fell asleep
and when I woke the bed was vacant,
neatly made.

I wake and hear the double calls once more:
sunbirds in a bush
and then the cry of starlings –
surely they are real this time
or do I long for imitation,
a greed of mimicry,
humour that makes art?

The lawns unblur in sun,
the trees become clear-cut:
I hear each sound give way to sound
and then once more a bubbling laugh
that only just could be a dove,
is human only by its fun and craft.
From the street I hear them shout goodbye.
A shadow crawls across my chair,
a touch of cold,
and yet the green is now so vivid, quickly bright,
amid the smoke of dusk.

Suddenly intense the silence floods the colour
And nothing sings in the hush.

FOR REBECCA, BORN AT MIDWINTER

Cockcrow at midwinter dark, air moving,
and then a slow
incantation from each tree,
as when the light comes slowly, crossing
centuries of dark on dark moving, slowly
the candour of the sun, as water
almost pauses for the brim, waiting
one slow moment, then goes beyond
a hesitation not its own,
steeping a new element,
so the light, so the fire
on water, earth and air: slow
the genesis.

Into each trick
of your head,
deft heiress, into
each cry
or reaching out
your fingers make,
each glance that blurs
about our awe,
come the centuries:
the spirit and mortality,
the virtue of our kind,
come random through
the strict inheritance,
the wide
deep ending of our past.

I watch you now and watch
how once a saint bent with your knee,
ghost-cosseted: and I may feel
the mad or innocent

throbbing in your pulse
or think that one who paints
an orange beast upon a rock
lingers in your smile. Newly-born,
here are those they hanged
and those who brought the harvest in:
the men at battle, grinning,
who learned the dialect of death,
who now lie buried, blank,
beneath the peat or bush.
It was for you the women died,
who, starved, and sick with hate,
have you for triumph now, you
once more their birth. Here
is ghostly policy and rage,
the labour and the knowledge.
O small thing, made, that lies
within your mother's arms,
you are the coming from, and all
that is to be.

Small and yet
a thing that bubbles
in itself, considering
itself: is godly
in its way, its
knowledge of the path
to take, the openings
of fate: and it will lose
that blest
and vague
perfection,
that impotent serenity,
will, in itself
and as itself, choose
just what to know,

at what
expense,
will find
the posture fit
for day and night,
a fresh dexterity
of hand and heart, new
reachings of the will, within,
without.

This shortest day in which
we saw you first
will send its light and shadow
through long seasons
of your own. Sleep now,
granddaughter, sleep
in the sanctity of birth:
you hold within your fist
the blessing and the curse,
all growing and all blight.
Hold your testament,
hold it as you must
within a fist
as blind and potent as a nut,
hold us,
all those whom Adam
or the older gods begat.

ETRUSCAN GIRL

It is a moving thing
to see in this figure
how the maker
has shown the girl
or young woman
plaiting her hair
so that the arm and fingers
as they move,
the tress itself,
are one piece in the clay,
fused, that no part
of the model should crack
in the oven,
that no part of the moment
be lost.

Just two foot high –
it might have been
an image for her tomb:
but who knows that
or anything
about this girl
who has no name,
no story? Even
the tongue she spoke
is blocked, obscure:
dust upon dust,
twenty five centuries,
annulling
all memory.

And the figure half turns
to stare at me,
as though I
could give a name:
as though death did not
repeal identity,
as though there were
a body there,
a spirit that I must see,
clearly.

And I try to imagine
those who called
the craftsman in,
the maker,
saying to him:
You knew   , you knew her well,
make her for us, make her
as we knew her in this life.

And it was
as he had seen her last,
sitting outside the house,
debonair in the morning,
plaiting her hair in the sun,
the hands and fingers quickly
pushing in and out
so closely that
the moment and the movement
fused:
and the maker saw
that they were one.

In memoriam S.B.C.

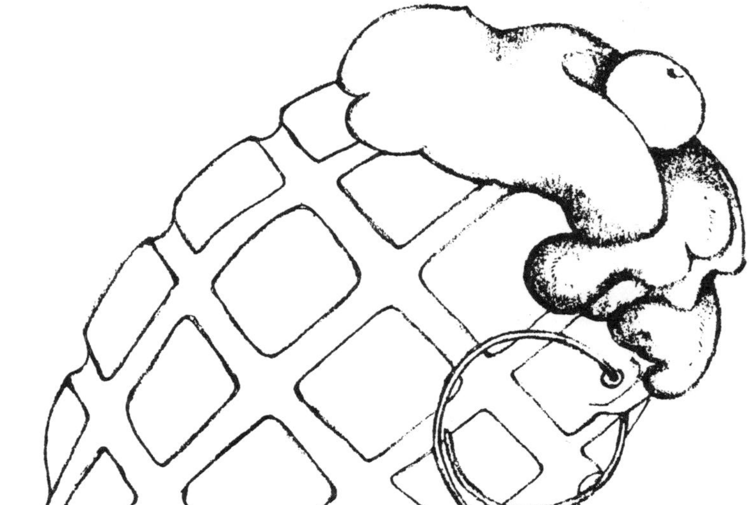

NOTES

I

Most of the poems in this section (1961-1972) were first published in *The Horizon Forty Miles Away* (Private printing, Johannesburg: 1973). A few were reprinted in *Today is not Different*. (See section II).

THE WALLS OF NALETALE

The ruins of Naletale are in the southern part of the Gweru district of Zimbabwe. They comprise a long wall decorated with chevron-patterned stones and this encircles a great dome of granite. There is a deep resonating hole or funnel formed in the rock. The ruin complex was most probably built by the Rozvi people at the end of the seventeenth or during the eighteenth century.

When I visited the site in the summer of 1964, I was shown around by an old man who talked of the past, of his ancestors, with a sort of genial but raucous awe. As I remember it, the bush around the ruins was verdant and stridulant with the noises of insects.

DEVILS

From time to time I have been asked if the figures in this poem represent any specific person. I can only say that 'Belmotto' was distantly inspired by H.F. Verwoerd and that 'Alexander' was vaguely based on John Harris, the 'Station Bomber'. Written in August 1964, the poem reflects anxiety about the political situation and the ambiguities, complacencies perhaps, of my position as a liberal.

THE ESTUARY

Like 'Devils' this poem also mirrors my disquiet about the political happenings in South Africa in 1964. The background is, however, Moçambique. The following three poems also derive from that country, but are set more specifically in 'LM', present-day Maputo. 'The War' was written in July 1971.

II

The poems in this section 1973-1979 are mainly taken from *Today is not Different* (David Philip, Cape Town: 1978).

FILIPPO ARGENTI

Filippo Argenti occurs in Canto VIII of Dante's *Inferno*. He was a Florentine nobleman of unbridled temper and arrogance – a type detested by the poet. He is immersed in the slime of the River Styx. As Virgil and Dante are crossing the river, Argenti tries to reach for their boat but Virgil repels him violently shouting 'Via costà con gli altri cani!' – 'Get away, go back to the other dogs!'. Later, the two poets see him being attacked by the other damned souls and see him biting at his own flesh.

1818. M. FRANCOIS LE VAILLANT...

The Frenchman, Francois le Vaillant, made one journey from Cape Town to the Eastern Cape and another to the Northern Cape and Namibia during the years 1780 to 1785. In 1796 he retired to his house at Sézanne, about 100 kilometres west of Paris and lived there until he died in 1824. In this poem he is portrayed reflecting upon his African travels, surrounded by his specimens of birds. Indeed, some of these were 'unofficial', in other words composite creatures created by his own imaginative taxonomy, and passed off as genuine in his *Oiseaux d'Afrique*, the first work to be devoted solely to African birds.

Many of Le Vaillant's claims and some of the anecdotes recounted in the volumes of his *Travels* are considered exaggerated if not downright lies. A case in point would be the story about loading his 'fusee' (or musket) 'with powder, wax and water' to shoot down birds so that their plumage would not be damaged by the ball or shot.

There are indications that Le Vaillant's collection, or 'cabinet' of birds attracted royal interest but nothing seems to have come of this. In any case, the Revolution intervened and he was imprisoned during the Reign of Terror in 1793. He was freed in July 1794, on the fall of Robespierre. The fact that many of the editions of the *Oiseaux d' Afrique* are stamped with the Napoleonic eagle seems to point to the fact that the Emperor played some part in their publication.

Le Vaillant admired the philosopher, Jean-Jacques Rousseau so ardently that he named a son after him. His *Travels* too are suffused with Rousseauesque sentiments. His noble savagery, in particular, is vividly displayed in the meeting with the Gonaqua tribe in the Eastern Cape and is overwhelmingly evident in his dalliance with a maiden he called Narina. Hence, also, his naming of a shy but beautiful bird the 'Narina Trogan'.

THE FIRST HOURS

The Italian quotation is from Canto IX, lines 16-18, of the Purgatorio. Here Dante is talking about 'The hour near dawn when the swallow begins her sad songs, remembering perhaps, her ancient woes', then follow the lines printed above my poem: 'that time when our mind, on pilgrimage, is influenced more by the body than by reason and in its vision is almost divine'.

SEPTEMBER AT THE TUILERIES

This poem is an extravaganza, a celebration that arose from a visit to Paris in the mid-seventies. It is also an attempt to express some of my gratitude and admiration for the French writers and poets who taught me so much in my adolescent years. Rimbaud holds a special place in this process of learning and that is why words and phrases from his work occur in the course of this poem. For instance, the 'blond waterfalls' in the opening line derive from the *Illumination* entitled 'L'Aube' ('Je ris au wasserfall blond...'). Similarly, the references to being 'intact' and 'absolutely modern' can be found in *Une Saison en Enfer* in the sections 'Mauvais Sang' ('...moi, je suis intact, et ça m'est égal') and 'Adieu' ('Il faut être absolument moderne.') respectively.

Montesquieu's (1689-1755) satirical view of French society *Les Lettres Persanes* was published in 1721. Théophile Gautier (1811-1872) in his poem 'L'Art' urged his fellow Parnassian poets to 'carve, file and chisel' their work ('sculpte, lime, cisèle...').

MKULU KAKHULU

The title is a Zulu phrase meaning 'The Greatest' – 'The Big Boss'. The 'Freedom' is a unit of this imaginary country's currency. The poem was written after a visit to Malawi in 1976.

CATEMBE FERRY

Another 'LM' poem written in the early seventies. The ferry used to leave Lourenço Marques harbour during the day (hourly if I remember correctly) and sail to Catembe which was across the bay. There were small restaurants where you could eat the exquisite local prawns and drink Portuguese *vinho verde*.

JOHANNESBURG NOVEMBER

Written in November 1976 after the winter revolt in Soweto.

III

I have called the poems in this section (1974-1994) *Versions*. This means that I have tried to make a poem in English by using a poem in another language as my model or point of departure. Naturally, some of these versions will be closer to the original than others: for example, those that were made in collaboration with Phil du Plessis. The rest, such as the Dante, the Guilhem de Poitiers and the Mandelstam are much freer. Like Chapman, the seventeenth-century translator of Homer, I hope at least that 'I have rendered all things of importance, with answerable life and height to my Author, (though with some periphrasis without which no man can worthilie translate anie worthie Poet).'

THE AGE

According to the poet's wife, Nadezhda Mandelstam, in all the poems of this period (1923) the poet 'speaks either directly or obliquely about his own position in the new life', that is to say: the victory of the Revolution. In another poem of the same period he called himself 'a sick son of the age, with quick-lime in his blood'.

EASTER TRANSIT

This poem, original title 'Pase op Pad', comes from Phil du Plessis' collection *Ek sing waar ek staan: Poesie 1982-1984*. In 1985 he and I collaborated in making English versions of the book. Cecil Skotnes also contributed ten fine woodcuts.

TWO MARES

According to a contemporary source: 'The Count of Poitiers was one of the greatest lovers who ever lived and one of the greatest deceivers of women. He was a fine knight at arms and generous with his love. He knew well how to compose songs and then to sing them...' This poem has the title 'Devinalh'.

A GOD UNKNOWN

This version is based on Canto XXVI (lines 85-142) of Dante's *Inferno*. Dante with his guide, Virgil, have reached the eighth *bolgia* of Hell and here they come upon Ulysses, trapped in eternal fire, because he had been a 'false counsellor'. Speaking from inside the flame, Ulysses tells how, having left Circe's island, he sailed through the Mediterranean without making any attempt to return home to his family. When he reaches the present-day Straits of Gibraltar, he urges his men to sail on into the unknown ocean that lies ahead (the Atlantic).

They respond eagerly and after sailing south for five months a great island-mountain comes into sight. Unknown to the travellers, they are, in fact, looking at Purgatory.

But it is against God's law that these pre-Christian pagans should see or know of this place. He, therefore, sends a storm which sinks the ship and drowns them before they can come any closer.

AT THE CAFE SAN MARCO

The versions based on poems by Eugenio Montale come from different collections. The first six pieces starting with 'At the Cafe San Marco' ('Il mio cronometro svizzero ...') all derive from *Altri Versi e Poesie Disperse* (Mondadori, Milano: 1981). The next poem 'In the Garden' ('Nel giardino') is to be found in *Diario postumo* (Mondadori, Milano: 1991). The final three are from much earlier times: 'Wind on the Half-Moon' ('Vento sulla mezzaluna') dates from 1948, 'The Letter Unwritten' ('Su una lettera non scritta') is from 1940 and finally 'The House on the Frontier' ('La casa dei doganieri') goes right back to 1930.

QUARTET

The lines 'Four hacks, whipped bloody/in a shell-shaped square' refer to the Palio race held annually in the main piazza of Siena.

IV

This last section (1980-1994) contains the bulk of the poems published in *The White Hail in the Orchard* (David Philip, Cape Town: 1984). The remaining poems have not been collected before.

GRAMARY

'Gramarye or Gramary n. *Archaic.* magic, necromancy or occult learning. C14 from old French *gramaire* GRAMMAR.' – *Collins English Dictionary.*

HOMAGE TO DAVID LIVINGSTONE PHAKAMILE YALI-MANISI

A famous Xhosa *imbongi* or praise-singer.

The reference to vanishing in the second last line of the poem echoes the Xhosa phrase 'Ncincilili' – I disappear. It is Yali-Manisi's usual way of signalling the end of a performance. By sitting down amongst his audience he is no longer seen and has therefore 'vanished'.

LAURA

The Italian phrase is a line about Laura from a poem by Petrarch: 'and I see her go by, so sweet and so deadly'.

NATIVITY

The background to this poem does not refer to any specific landscape or painting. But clearly an Italian scene is suggested: Tuscan or Umbrian.

VENICE

The 'whore' in the second stanza can be seen in the celebrated painting by Carpaccio (1460-1526) of two Venetian ladies, sometimes entitled 'Two Courtesans'. The original is to be found in the Museo Correr in Venice.

I had recently suffered a heart attack when I wrote this poem in Venice. 'The city is drowning' – I was told. So the poem is a meditation on death.

ETRUSCAN GIRL

This image of an Etruscan girl can be seen in M. Palottino (ed), *Art of the Etruscans* (Thames & Hudson, London: 1955), p.118. It is described as 'Late second century B.C. Clay. Height 62 cm'. The accompanying text also states 'The twisted sleeves of the drapery are particularly striking, for they are exactly like the plaits of her hair; it is as if the interweaving of the plaiting hands were apparent in the material itself'.

OTHER SNAILPRESS WRITERS

Ken Barris
N H Brettell
Sue Clark
Peter E Clarke
Michael Cope
Phil du Plessis
Jane Fox
Marc Glaser
Esther Gravett
Alan James
Moira Lovell
Rod Mackenzie
Mzi Mahola
Sandra Meyer
Mteto Mzongwana
Mike Nicol
Karen Press
Jacques Prévert (in translation)
Heather Robertson
Jane Rosenthal
Walter Saunders
Damian Shaw
Augustine Shutte
Daniel Stolfi
Ian Tromp
Peter Wilhelm
Wendy Woodward

WITH MAYIBUYE BOOKS:

Keith Gottschalk
Tatamkhulu Afrika

WITH HOND:

Peter Kantey
Phil du Plessis

WITH RED KITE (CANADA):

Cherry Clayton

WITH CRANE RIVER:

C J Driver

The Animals Within

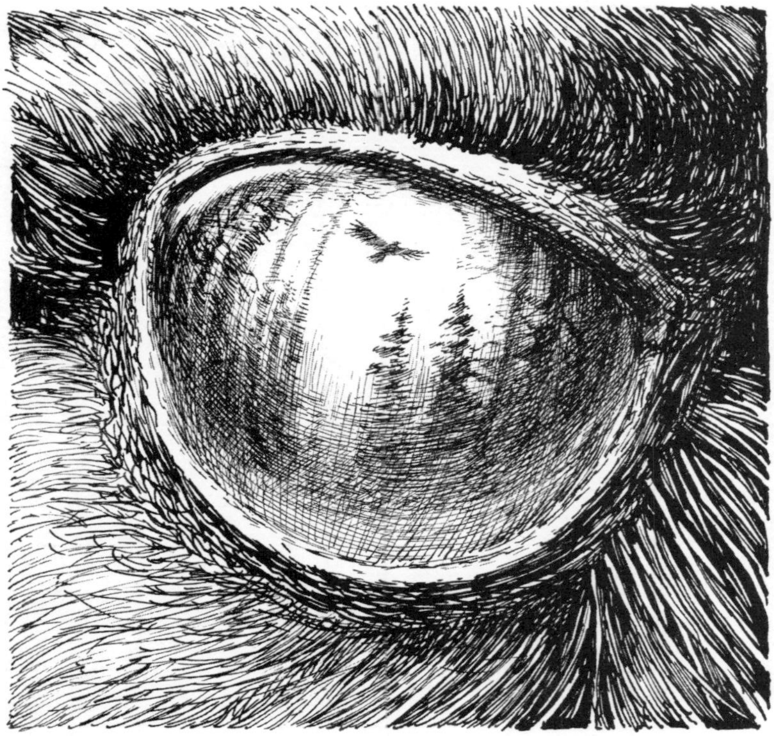

THE ANIMALS WITHIN

David Day

Illustrated by Alan Lee

Penumbra Press, 1984

This edition is limited to 1000 copies, of which the first one hundred are signed and numbered by the author.

Published by Penumbra Press, P.O. Box 340, Moonbeam, Ontario, Canada POL 1VO, in collaboration with Magus Publications, 23 Laurier Road, London, England, NW5, and with financial assistance from the Canada Council and the Ontario Arts Council.

ISBN 0 920806 61 9